for Kids only

365 Daily Devotions

Scripture quotations are taken from:

The Holy Bible, King James Version (KJV)

The Holy Bible, New International Version (NIV) Copyright © 1973, 1978, 1984, by International Bible Society. Used by permission of Zondervan Publishing House. All rights reserved.

The Holy Bible, New King James Version (NKJV) Copyright © 1982 by Thomas Nelson, Inc. Used by permission.

The New American Standard Bible®, (NASB) Copyright © 1960, 1962, 1963, 1968, 1971, 1972, 1973, 1975, 1977, 1995 by The Lockman Foundation. Used by permission.

Holy Bible, New Living Translation, (NLT)copyright © 1996. Used by permission of Tyndale House Publishers, Inc., Wheaton, Illinois 60189. All rights reserved.

The Message (MSG)- This edition issued by contractual arrangement with NavPress, a division of The Navigators, U.S.A. Originally published by NavPress in English as THE MESSAGE: The Bible in Contemporary Language copyright 2002-2003 by Eugene Peterson. All rights reserved.

New Century Version®. (NCV) Copyright © 1987, 1988, 1991 by Word Publishing, a division of Thomas Nelson, Inc. All rights reserved. Used by permission.

International Children's Bible®, New Century Version®. (ICB) Copyright © 1986, 1988, 1999 by Tommy Nelson™, a division of Thomas Nelson, Inc. All rights reserved. Used by permission.

The Holman Christian Standard Bible™ (HOLMAN CSB) Copyright © 1999, 2000, 2001 by Holman Bible Publishers. Used by permission.

Cover Design and Page Layout by Bart Dawson

ISBN-13 978-1-58334-458-3

ISBN-10 1-58334-458-6

Printed in the United States of America

for Kids only

365 Daily
Devotions

A Message to Parents

Perhaps your child's bookshelf is already filled with an interesting, spirit-lifting collection of children's books. If so, that means you're a thoughtful parent who understands the importance of reading to your young child. And if you treasure the time you spend reading to your youngster, this text can be an extremely important addition to your child's library.

This book (which is intended to be read by Christian parents to their young children) contains 365 brief chapters, one for each day of the year (plus an extra one for leap year). Many chapters have been taken from the popular "Little Book Devotions" series, a collection of kid-friendly essays on topics such as kindness, honesty, forgiveness, and self-control. Other chapters contain notable Bible verses which can be discussed—and perhaps memorized—by your child. Still other chapters contain "Big Ideas" which are easy to understand quotations from notable Christian thinkers.

If, during the coming year, you read this book to your child, you'll enjoy 365 different opportunities to share God's wisdom with your son or daughter, and that's a very good thing.

If you have been touched by God's love and His grace, then you know the joy that He has brought into your own life. Now it's your turn to share His message with the boy or girl whom He has entrusted to your care. Happy reading! And may God richly bless you and your family now and forever.

for Kids only

The World's Best Friend

Then Jesus said, "I am the bread that gives life.
Whoever comes to me will never be hungry,
and whoever believes in me will never be thirsty."

John 6:35 NCV

Who's the best friend this world has ever had? Jesus, of course! When you invite Him into your heart, Jesus will be your friend, too . . . your friend forever.

Jesus has offered to share the gifts of everlasting life and everlasting love with the world . . . and with you. If you make mistakes, He'll still be your friend. If you behave badly, He'll still love you. If you feel sorry or sad, He can help you feel better.

Jesus wants you to have a happy, healthy life. He wants you to be generous and kind. He wants you to follow His example. And the rest is up to you. You can do it! And with a friend like Jesus, you will.

Kid's Tip: What a friend you have in Jesus: Jesus loves you, and He offers you eternal life with Him in heaven. Welcome Him into your heart. Now!

Feeling Better

A wise person is patient. He will be honored if he
ignores a wrong done against him.
Proverbs 19:11 ICB

Is forgiving someone else an easy thing for you
to do or a hard thing? If you're like most people,
forgiving others can be hard, Hard, HARD! But even
if you're having a very hard time forgiving someone,
you can do it if you talk things over with your
parents, and if you talk things over with God.

Do you find forgiveness difficult? Talk about it
and pray about it. You'll feel better when you do.

When God forgives, He forgets.
He buries our sins in the sea and puts a sign on
the shore saying, "No Fishing Allowed."

Corrie ten Boom

Solomon Says . . . Be Kind!

A kind person is doing himself a favor.
But a cruel person brings trouble upon himself.
Proverbs 11:17 ICB

King Solomon wrote most of the Book of Proverbs; in it, he gave us wonderful advice for living wisely. Solomon warned that unkind behavior leads only to trouble, but kindness is its own reward.

The next time you're tempted to say an unkind word, remember Solomon. He was one of the wisest men who ever lived, and he knew that it's always better to be kind. And now, you know it, too.

Kid's Tip: Kindness every day: Kindness should be part of our lives every day, not just on the days when we feel good. Don't try to be kind some of the time, and don't try to be kind to some of the people you know. Instead, try to be kind all of the time, and try to be kind to all the people you know. Remember, the Golden Rule starts with you!

Today's Ideas About
God's Plans

Here are two important ideas. Take a few minutes to talk to your mom or dad about what these quotations mean.

When the dream of our heart is one that God has planted there, a strange happiness flows into us. At that moment, all of the spiritual resources of the universe are released to help us. Our praying is then at one with the will of God and becomes a channel for the Creator's purposes for us and our world.

Catherine Marshall

God is at work; He is in full control; He is in the midst of whatever has happened, is happening, and will happen.

Charles Swindoll

The Best Day

This is the day the LORD has made.
We will rejoice and be glad in it.
Psalm 118:24 NLT

What is the best day to celebrate life? This one! Today and every day should be a time for celebration as we think about all the things God has done for us.

Today, as you take time to count your blessings, enjoy yourself. This day (like every other one) is a gift from your Heavenly Father . . . SO CELEBRATE!

Kid's Tip: Share the Good News: While you're celebrating life, don't try and keep the celebration to yourself. Let other people know why you're rejoicing, and don't be bashful about telling them how they can rejoice, too.

Your Attitude

Make your own attitude that of Christ Jesus.

Philippians 2:5 Holman CSB

What's an attitude? The word "attitude" means "the way that you think." And don't forget this: your attitude is important.

Your attitude can make you happy or sad, grumpy or glad, joyful or mad. And, your attitude doesn't just control the way that you think; it also controls how you behave. If you have a good attitude, you'll behave well. And if you have a bad attitude, you're more likely to misbehave.

Have you spent any time thinking about the way that you think? Do you pay much attention to your attitude? Hopefully so! After all, a good attitude is better than a bad one . . . lots better.

You have more control over your attitude than you think. So do your best to make your attitude a good attitude. One way you can do that is by learning about Jesus and about His attitude toward life. When you do, you'll learn that it's always better to think good thoughts, and it's always better to do good things. Always!

Sharing Your Stuff

In every way I've shown you that by laboring like
this, it is necessary to help the weak and to keep in
mind the words of the Lord Jesus, for He said,
"It is more blessed to give than to receive."

Acts 20:35 Holman CSB

A re you one of those kids who is lucky enough
to have a closet filled up with stuff? If so, it's
probably time to share some of it.

When your mom or dad says it's time to clean up
your closet and give some things away, don't be sad.
Instead of whining, think about all the children who
could enjoy the things that you don't use very much.
And while you're at it, think about what Jesus might
tell you to do if He were here. Jesus would tell
you to share generously and cheerfully. And that's
exactly what you should do!

Kid's Tip: Finding loving homes for clothes and toys:
your parents can help you find younger children who
need the clothes and toys that you've outgrown.

Finish What You Begin

We say they are happy because they did not give up.
You have heard about Job's patience,
and you know the Lord's purpose for him in the end.
You know the Lord is full of mercy and is kind.

James 5:11 NCV

Jesus finished what He began, and so should you. Jesus didn't give in, and neither should you. Jesus did what was right, and so should you.

Are you facing something that is hard for you to do? If so, you may be tempted to quit. If so, remember this: whatever your problem, God can handle it. Your job is to keep working until He does.

Kid's Tip: If things don't work out at first, don't quit. If you never try, you'll never know how good you can be.

Today's Ideas About
Your Troubles and Your Prayers

Here are two important ideas. Take a few minutes
to talk to your mom or dad about what these
quotations mean.

When problems threaten to engulf us,
we must do what believers have always done,
turn to the Lord for encouragement and solace.
As Psalm 46:1 states, "God is our refuge and
strength, an ever-present help in trouble."

Shirley Dobson

We sometimes fear to bring our troubles to God,
because they must seem so small to him who sitteth
on the circle of the earth. But, if they are large
enough to vex and endanger our welfare,
they are large enough to touch his heart of love.

R. A. Torrey

Try to Memorize This Verse

God loves a cheerful giver.

2 Corinthians 9:7 NIV

This is an important Bible verse.
Practice saying it several times. And then, talk to
mom or dad about exactly what the verse means . . .

A Tip for Parents: Talk to your child about . . .

The joy of giving

Self-Control and Patience

All athletes practice strict self-control.
They do it to win a prize that will fade away,
but we do it for an eternal prize.
1 Corinthians 9:25 NLT

The Book of Proverbs tells us that self-control and patience are very good things to have. But for most of us, self-control and patience can also be very hard things to learn.

Are you having trouble being patient? And are you having trouble slowing down long enough to think before you act? If so, remember that self-control takes practice, and lots of it, so keep trying. And if you make a mistake, don't be too upset. After all, if you're going to be a really patient person, you shouldn't just be patient with others; you should also be patient with yourself.

Your thoughts are the determining factor
as to whose mold you are conformed to.
Control your thoughts and you control
the direction of your life.
Charles Stanley

Parents Can Help

The one who lives with integrity is righteous;
his children who come after him will be happy.

Proverbs 20:7 Holman CSB

Whenever you want to get better at something, you should always be willing to let your parents help out in any way they can. After all, your parents want you to become the very best person you can be. So, if you want to become better at controlling your own behavior, ask your parents to help. How can they help out? By reminding you to slow down and think about things before you do them—not after. It's as simple as that.

Kid's Tip: Your parents love you and want to help you. Their job is to help . . . your job is to listen carefully to the things they say.

Today's Ideas About Heaven

Here are two important ideas. Take a few minutes to talk to your mom or dad about what these quotations mean.

What joy that the Bible tells us the great comfort that the best is yet to be. Our outlook goes beyond this world.

Corrie ten Boom

Earth's best is only a dim reflection and a preliminary rendering of the glory that will one day be revealed.

Joni Eareckson Tada

Celebrate!

Celebrate God all day, every day.
I mean, revel in him!
Philippians 4:4 MSG

Do you feel like celebrating? Hopefully so! Are you expecting God to do wonderful things? Hopefully so! Are you happy about your family, your friends, and your church? Hopefully so! After all, God loves you, and that fact should make you very happy indeed. So treat this day as a big celebration . . . because that's exactly what it should be.

Enjoy the adventure of receiving God guidance.
Taste it, revel in it, appreciate the fact
that the journey is often a lot more exciting
than arriving at the destination.
Bill Hybels

Kid's Tip: Today is a cause for celebration: Psalm 118:24 has clear instructions for the coming day: "This is the day which the LORD has made; let us rejoice and be glad in it." Plan your day—and your life—accordingly.

Starting Your Day

It is good to give thanks to the Lord, to sing praises
to the Most High. It is good to proclaim
your unfailing love in the morning,
your faithfulness in the evening.

Psalm 92:1-2 NLT

How do you start your day? Do you sleep till the
last possible moment without giving a single
thought to God? Hopefully, that's not the case. If
you're smart, you'll start your day with a prayer of
thanks to your Heavenly Father.

Each new day is a gift from God, and if you're
wise, you'll spend a few quiet moments thanking the
Giver. It's a wonderful way to start your day.

A child of God should never leave his bedroom
in the morning without being on
good terms with God.

C. H. Spurgeon

Kid's Tip: Make an appointment with God and keep
it: Bible study and prayer should be at the top of
your to-do list, not the bottom.

Setting an Example

Set an example of good works yourself,
with integrity and dignity in your teaching.
Titus 2:7 Holman CSB

The Bible says that you are "the light that gives light to the world." The Bible also says that you should live in a way that lets other people understand what it means to be a good person. And of course, learning to share is an important part of being a good person.

What kind of "light" have you been giving off? Hopefully, you have been a good example for everybody to see. Why? Because the world needs all the light it can get, and that includes your light, too!

Kid's Tip: Think about the ways that your behavior impacts your family and friends.

Try to Memorize This Verse

For God so loved the world that
He gave His only begotten Son,
that whoever believes in Him should
not perish but have everlasting life.

John 3:16 NKJV

This is an important Bible verse.
Practice saying it several times. And then, talk to
mom or dad about exactly what the verse means . . .

Parent Tip: Talk to Your Child About . . .

God's infinite love

What a Friend

And I am convinced that nothing can ever separate us from his love. Whether we are high above the sky or in the deepest ocean, nothing in all creation will ever be able to separate us from the love of God that is revealed in Christ Jesus our Lord.

Romans 8:38-39 NLT

Perhaps you've heard these words before: "Jesus loves me, this I know, for the Bible tells me so." Of course, these words can be found in the song "Jesus Loves Me." It's a wonderful song that should remind you of something very important: Jesus loves you very much.

When you invite Jesus to become your friend, He will do it . . . and He'll be your friend forever. If you make mistakes, He'll still be your friend. If you misbehave, He'll still love you. If you feel sorry or sad, He can help you feel better.

Yes, Jesus loves you more than you know. And when you welcome Him into your heart, you will be blessed now and forever.

Kid's Tip: Jesus loves you . . . His love is amazing, it's wonderful, and it's meant for you.

Love Everybody

But love ye your enemies, and do good,
and lend, hoping for nothing again; and your reward
shall be great, and ye shall be the children
of the Highest . . . .
Luke 6:35 KJV

It's easy to love people who have been nice to you, but it's very hard to love people who have treated you badly. Still, Jesus instructs us to treat both our friends and our enemies with kindness and respect.

Are you having problems being nice to someone? Is there someone you know whom you don't like very much? Remember that Jesus not only forgave His enemies, He also loved them . . . and so should you.

Kid's Tip: How hard is it to love your enemies? You'll never know until you try . . . so try!

An Example for Others

We're Christ's representatives. God uses us to
persuade men and women to drop their differences
and enter into God's work of making things
right between them. We're speaking for
Christ himself now: Become friends with God;
he's already a friend with you.

2 Corinthians 5:20 MSG

What kind of example are you? Are you the kind
of person who shows other people what it
means to be kind and forgiving? Hopefully so!!!

How hard is it to say a kind word? Not very! How
hard is it to accept someone's apology? Usually not
too hard. So today, be a good example for others
to follow. Because God needs people, like you, who
are willing to stand up and be counted for Him. And
that's exactly the kind of example you should always
try to be.

Kid's Tip: Your behavior speaks volumes about your
relationship with God.

Day 21

Try to Memorize This Verse

**It is good and pleasant
when God's people live together in peace!**

Psalm 133:1 NCV

This is an important Bible verse.
Practice saying it several times. And then, talk to
mom or dad about exactly what the verse means . . .

A Tip for Parents: Talk to your child about . . .

How to live with family and friends

The Roadblock

Those who show mercy to others are happy,
because God will show mercy to them.

Matthew 5:7 NCV

If you're unwilling to forgive other people, you're building a roadblock between yourself and God. And the less you're willing to forgive, the bigger your roadblock.

If you really want to forgive someone, pray for that person. And then pray for yourself by asking God to help you forgive. Don't expect forgiveness to be easy or quick, but with God as your helper, you can forgive . . . and you will.

God calls upon the loved not just to love
but to be loving. God calls upon the forgiven
not just to forgive but to be forgiving.

Beth Moore

Thanks for the Memories

I give thanks to my God
for every remembrance of you.
Philippians 1:3 Holman CSB

In his letter to the Philippians, Paul wrote to his distant friends saying that he thanked God every time He remembered them. We, too, should thank God for the family and friends He has brought into our lives.

Today, let's give thanks to God for all the people who love us, for brothers and sisters, parents and grandparents, aunts and uncles, cousins, and friends. And then, as a way of thanking God, let's obey Him by being especially kind to our loved ones. They deserve it, and so does He.

The best times in life are made a thousand times better when shared with a dear friend.
Luci Swindoll

God Solves Problems

Since God assured us, "I'll never let you down,
never walk off and leave you," we can
boldly quote, God is there, ready to help;
I'm fearless no matter what.
Who or what can get to me?

Hebrews 13:5-6 MSG

Do you have a problem that you haven't been
able to solve? Welcome to the club! Life is full
of problems that don't have easy solutions. But if
you have a problem that you can't solve, there is
something you can do: turn that problem over to
God. He can handle it.

God has a way of solving our problems if we let
Him; our job is to let Him. God can handle things
that we can't. And the sooner we turn our concerns
over to Him, the sooner He will go to work solving
those troubles that are simply too big for us to
handle.

If you're worried or discouraged, pray about it.
And ask your parents and friends to pray about it,
too. And then stop worrying because no problem is
too big for God; not even yours.

No Regrets

Don't let your spirit rush to be angry,
for anger abides in the heart of fools.

Ecclesiastes 7:9 Holman CSB

When you're angry, you will be tempted to say things and do things that you'll regret later. So don't do them! Instead of doing things in a hurry, slow down long enough to calm yourself down.

Jesus does not intend that you strike out against other people, and He doesn't intend that your heart be troubled by anger. Your heart should instead be filled with love, just like Jesus' heart was . . . and is!

Kid's Tip: Time Out!: If you become angry, the time to step away from the situation is before you say unkind words or do unkind things—not after. It's perfectly okay to place yourself in "time out" until you can calm down.

The Right Time

He has made everything beautiful in its time.
He has also set eternity in the hearts of men;
yet they cannot fathom what God has done
from beginning to end.

Ecclesiastes 3:11 NIV

Sometimes, the hardest thing to do is to wait. This is especially true when we're in a hurry and when we want things to happen now, if not sooner! But God's plan does not always happen in the way that we would like or at the time of our own choosing. Still, God always knows best.

Sometimes, even though we may want something very badly, we must still be patient and wait for the right time to get it. And the right time, of course, is determined by God, not by us.

Kid's Tip: Even when you want events to unfold according to your own timetable, it is important to trust God's timetable.

Today's Ideas About
The Words You Speak

Here are two important ideas. Take a few minutes to talk to your mom or dad about what these quotations mean.

I still believe we ought to talk about Jesus. The old country doctor of my boyhood days always began his examination by saying, "Let me see your tongue." That's a good way to check a Christian: the tongue test. Let's hear what he is talking about.

Vance Havner

Change the heart, and you change the speech.

Warren Wiersbe

When Homework Should Be Done

We can't afford to waste a minute, must not squander these precious daylight hours in frivolity and indulgence, in sleeping around and dissipation, in bickering and grabbing everything in sight. Get out of bed and get dressed! Don't loiter and linger, waiting until the very last minute. Dress yourselves in Christ, and be up and about!

Romans 13:13-14 MSG

Sooner or later, you'll start getting homework, and when that day comes, you'd better be ready because that's when you'll really need lots of self-control! Usually, homework isn't hard to do, but it takes time. And sometimes, we'd rather be doing other things (like playing outside or watching TV). But, when we put off our homework until the last possible minute, we make it hard on ourselves.

Instead of putting off your homework, do it first. Then, you'll have the rest of your time to have fun—and you won't have to worry about all that homework.

Telling the Truth

Don't ever forget kindness and truth.
Wear them like a necklace.
Write them on your heart as if on a tablet.

Proverbs 3:3 NCV

When we're dishonest, we make ourselves unhappy and we let other people down. It's easy to see that lies always cause far more problems than they solve. Lies, no matter what size, are never part of God's plan for our lives, so we must tell the truth about everything.

Have you ever said something that wasn't true? When you did, were you sorry for what you had said? Probably so.

Happiness and honesty always go hand in hand. But it's up to you to make sure that you go hand in hand with them! And besides, when you always tell the truth, you don't have to try and remember what it was that you said!

A lie is like a snowball: the further you roll it, the bigger it becomes.

Martin Luther

Kindness Is a Choice

Love is patient; love is kind.

1 Corinthians 13:4 Holman CSB

Kindness is a choice. Sometimes, when we feel happy or hopeful, we find it easy to be kind. Other times, when we are sad or tired, we may find it much harder to be kind. But the Bible teaches us to be kind, even when we don't feel like it.

So do everybody (including yourself) a big favor: try to be kind all the time. It's the smart choice and the right thing to do.

Kid's Tip: Kindness every day: Kindness should be part of our lives every day, not just on the days when we feel good. And remember: small acts of kindness can make a big difference.

Do the Right Thing . . .
And the Kind Thing

Let everyone see that you are gentle and kind.
The Lord is coming soon.

Philippians 4:5 NCV

Sometimes, it's so much easier to do the wrong thing than it is to do the right thing, especially when we're tired or frustrated. But, doing the wrong thing almost always leads to trouble. And sometimes, it leads to BIG trouble.

When you do the right thing, you don't have to worry about what you did or what you said. But, when you do the wrong thing, you'll be worried that someone will find out. So do the right thing, which, by the way, also happens to be the kind thing. You'll be glad you did, and so will other people!

When you launch an act of kindness
out into the crosswinds of life,
it will blow kindness back to you.

Dennis Swanberg

Today's Ideas About
Helping Others

Here are two important ideas. Take a few minutes to talk to your mom or dad about what these quotations mean.

Encouraging others means helping people, looking for the best in them, and trying to bring out their positive qualities.

John Maxwell

Make it a rule, and pray to God to help you to keep it, never, if possible, to lie down at night without being able to say: "I have made one human being at least a little wiser, or a little happier, or at least a little better this day."

Charles Kingsley

Learning the Importance of Obedience

You must follow the Lord your God and fear Him.
You must keep His commands and listen to His voice;
you must worship Him and remain faithful to Him.

Deuteronomy 13:4 Holman CSB

When you learn to control your actions and your words, you will find it easier to obey your parents, your teachers, and your Father in heaven. Why? Because in order to be an obedient person, you must first learn how to control yourself— otherwise, you won't be able to obey very well, even when you want to.

When you learn the importance of obedience, you'll soon discover that good things happen when you behave yourself. And the sooner you learn to listen and obey, the sooner those good things will start happening.

Kid's Tip: Obeying God? Yes Sir! What about the rules you learn about in the Bible? Well, those aren't just any old rules—they're God's rules. And you should behave—and obey—accordingly.

Want More Patience?
God Can Help!

Smart people are patient; they will be honored
if they ignore insults.

Proverbs 19:11 NCV

Are you a perfectly patient person? If so, feel
free to skip the rest of this page. But if you're
not, here's something to think about: If you really
want to become a more patient person, God is ready
and willing to help.

God is always ready to help you become a better
person. In fact, the Bible promises that when you
sincerely seek God's help, He will give you the things
you need. So, if you want to become a more patient
person, bow your head and start praying about it.
Then, rest assured that with God's help, you can
change for the better . . . and you will!

Kid's Tip: Even when you don't understand the
circumstances that confront you, strive to wait
patiently while serving the Lord.

Christ's Peace

Peace I leave with you. My peace I give to you.
I do not give to you as the world gives.
Your heart must not be troubled or fearful.

John 14:27 Holman CSB

The beautiful words of John 14:27 remind us that Jesus offers us peace, not as the world gives, but as He alone gives. We, as believers, can accept His peace or ignore it. When we accept the peace of Jesus Christ into our hearts, our lives are changed forever, and we become more loving, patient Christians.

Christ's peace is offered freely; it has been already been paid for; it is ours for the asking. So let us ask . . . and then share.

Kid's Tip: King David knew that God could restore his sense of peace . . . so he prayed. And so should you.

When Things Go Wrong

I do not consider myself yet to have taken hold
of it. But one thing I do: Forgetting what is behind
and straining toward what is ahead, I press on
toward the goal to win the prize for which God
has called me heavenward in Christ Jesus.

Philippians 3:13-14 NIV

When things don't turn out right, it's easy for
most of us to give up. But usually, it's wrong.
Why are we tempted to give up so quickly? Perhaps
it's because we're afraid that we might embarrass
ourselves if we tried hard but didn't succeed.

Here's something to remember: if you're having a
little trouble getting something done, don't get mad,
don't get frustrated, don't get discouraged, and
don't give up. Just keep trying . . . and keep believing
in yourself.

When you try hard—and keep trying hard—you
can do amazing things . . . but if you quit at the first
sign of trouble, you'll miss out. So here's a good rule
to follow: when you have something that you want to
finish, be brave enough (and wise enough) to finish it
. . . you'll feel better about yourself when you do.

Are You Feeling Upset or Worried? Pray About It!

I want men everywhere to lift up holy hands in prayer, without anger or disputing.

1 Timothy 2:8 NIV

If you're feeling upset, what should you do? Well, you should talk to your parents and there's something else you can do: you can pray about it.

If there is a person you don't like, you should pray for a forgiving heart. If there is something you're worried about, you should ask God to give you comfort. And as you pray more, you'll discover that God is always near and that He's always ready to hear from you. So don't worry about things; pray about them. God is waiting patiently to hear from you . . . and He's ready to listen NOW!

Kid's Tip: One way to make sure that your heart is in tune with God is to pray often. The more you talk to God, the more He will talk to you.

When We Don't Understand

Immediately the father of the child cried out
and said with tears,
"Lord, I believe; help my unbelief!"
Mark 9:24 NKJV

Even a good man like Moses couldn't always understand the mysteries of God's plans. And neither can we. Sometimes, people who do nothing wrong get sick; sometimes, innocent people are hurt; sometimes, bad things happen to very good people. And just like Moses, we can't always understand why.

But the good news is this: We will have an eternity to have all our questions answered when we get to heaven. And until then, we've simply got to trust God.

Kid's Tip: If you're afraid to raise your hand and ask a question, remember this . . . if you don't understand something, lots of other people in the classroom probably don't understand it, either. So you'll be doing everybody a big favor if you raise your hand and ask your question.

Safety Matters

The prudent see danger and take refuge,
but the simple keep going and suffer from it.
Proverbs 27:12 NIV

Self-control and safety go hand in hand. Why?
Because a big part of self-control is looking
around and thinking things through before you do
something that you might regret later.

Remember the saying "Look before you leap"?
Well if you want to live safely and happily, you
should look very carefully before you decide
whether or not to leap. After all, it's easy to leap,
but once you're in the middle of your jump, it's too
late to leap back!

Kid's Tip: Don't complain about safety: whether it's
a fire drill at school or wearing seat belts in the
family car, don't whine, complain, or resist. When
grown-ups are trying to keep you safe, your job is to
help them do it!

Today's Ideas About
Celebrating Today

Here are two important ideas. Take a few minutes to talk to your mom or dad about what these quotations mean.

Don't waste today's time cluttering up tomorrow's opportunities with yesterday's troubles.

Barbara Johnson

With each new dawn, life delivers a package to your front door, rings your doorbell, and runs.

Charles Swindoll

Making Other People Feel Better

Be gracious in your speech. The goal is to bring out
the best in others in a conversation,
not put them down, not cut them out.

Colossians 4:6 MSG

Do you like for people to say kind words to you?
Of course you do! And that's exactly how other
people feel, too. That's why it's so important to say
things that make people feel better, not worse.

Your words can help people . . . or not. Make
certain that you're the kind of person who says
helpful things, not hurtful things. And, make sure
that you're the kind of person who helps other
people feel better about themselves, not worse.

Kid's Tip: When in doubt, use the Golden Rule to
help you decide what to say: If you wouldn't like
for somebody to say it about you, don't say it about
them!

When to Stop
Temper Tantrums

A hot-tempered person starts fights
and gets into all kinds of sin.
Proverbs 29:22 NLT

Temper tantrums are one of the silliest ways to lose self-control. Why? Because when we lose our temper, we say things that we shouldn't say, and we do things that we shouldn't do. And to make matters worse, once the tantrum is over, we usually feel embarrassed or worse.

The Bible tells us that it isn't very smart to become angry. That's why we should learn to stop temper tantrums before they get started.

Kid's Tip: If you become angry, the time to step away from the situation is before you say unkind words or do unkind things—not after. So it's perfectly okay to place yourself in "time out" until you can calm down.

Happy Thoughts

Those who are pure in their thinking are happy,
because they will be with God.
Matthew 5:8 NCV

Do you try to think the kind of thoughts that
make you happy, not sad? The Bible says that
you should.

Do you try to think about things that are true
and right? The Bible says that you should.

Do you turn away from bad thoughts—and away
from people who misbehave? The Bible says that you
should.

The Bible instructs you to guard your thoughts
against things that are hurtful or wrong. So
remember this: when you turn away from the bad
thoughts and bad people, you've made a very wise
choice.

Kid's Tip: It is important to focus your thoughts on
the positive aspects of life, not the negative ones.

Big Rewards When You Do the Right Thing

Do you want to be counted wise, to build
a reputation for wisdom? Here's what you do:
Live well, live wisely, live humbly.
It's the way you live, not the way you talk,
that counts.

James 3:13 MSG

If you open up a dictionary, you'll see that the word "wisdom" means "using good judgement, and knowing what is true." But there's more to it than that. It's not enough to know what's right—if you want to be wise, you must also do what's right.

The Bible promises that when you do smart things, you'll earn big rewards, so slow down and think about things before you do them, not after.

Kid's Tip: Learning about God's truth is "head knowledge" and it is incomplete. Learning and doing God's truth is "head-and-heart knowledge" . . . and it is complete.

Lies Can Lead to Trouble

Your heart must not be troubled.
Believe in God; believe also in Me.
John 14:1 Holman CSB

When we tell a lie, trouble starts. Lots of trouble. But when we tell the truth—and nothing but the truth—we stop Old Man Trouble in his tracks.

When we always tell the truth, we make our worries smaller, not bigger. And that's precisely what God wants us to do.

So, if you'd like to have fewer worries and more happiness, abide by this simple rule: tell the truth, the whole truth, and nothing but the truth. When you do, you'll make many of your worries disappear altogether. And that's the truth!

Kid's Tip: Categorize Your Worries: Carefully divide your areas of concern into two categories: those things you can control and those you cannot control. Once you've done so, spend your time working to resolve the things you can control, and entrust everything else to God.

ay's Ideas About
Forgiveness

Here are two important ideas. Take a few minutes
to talk to your mom or dad about what these
quotations mean.

We are products of our past,
but we don't have to be prisoners of it.
God specializes in giving people
a fresh start.

Rick Warren

There are some facts that will
never change. One fact is that you are
forgiven. He sees you better than
you see yourself. And that is
a glorious fact of your life.

Max Lucado

Contentment Now

Keep your lives free from the love of money
and be content with what you have,
because God has said, "Never will I leave you;
never will I forsake you."

Hebrews 13:5 NIV

Where can we find contentment? Is it a result of being wealthy or famous? Nope. Genuine contentment is a gift from God to those who trust Him and follow His commandments.

If we don't find contentment in God, we will never find it anywhere else. But, if we seek Him and obey Him, we will be blessed with joyful, peaceful, meaningful lives. When God dwells at the center of our lives, peace and contentment will belong to us just as surely as we belong to God.

Kid's Tip: Be contented where you are, even if it's not exactly where you want to end up: Think about it like this: God has something wonderful in store for you—and remember that God's timing is perfect—so be patient, trust God, do your best, and expect the best.

A Forever Love

I am the good shepherd.
The good shepherd lays down his life
for the sheep.

John 10:11 NIV

You've probably heard the song "Jesus Loves Me." And exactly how much does He love you? He loves you so much that He gave His life so that you might live forever with Him in heaven.

How can you repay Christ's love? By accepting Him into your heart and by obeying His rules. When you do, He will love you and bless you today, tomorrow, and forever.

Jesus is all compassion. He never betrays us.

Catherine Marshall

A Helping Hand

Hatred stirs up trouble, but love forgives all wrongs.
Proverbs 10:12 NCV

Sometimes, young people can be very mean. They can make fun of other people, and when they do so, it's wrong. Period.

As Christians, we should be kind to everyone. And, if other kids say unkind things to a child or make fun of him or her, it's up to us to step in, like the Good Samaritan, and lend a helping hand.

Today and every day, be a person who is known for your kindness, not for your cruelty. That's how God wants you to behave. Period.

Kid's Tip: Stand Up for What's Right! If one of your friends is being cruel, unkind, or discourteous, don't join in! Instead, stand up for the people who need your help. Remember what Jesus said: when you help people in need, you're helping Him, too. (Matthew 25:40)

Hit a Homerun

Don't be afraid. Only believe.

Mark 5:36 Holman CSB

His fans called him the "Sultan of Swat." He was Babe Ruth, the baseball player who set records for home runs and strikeouts. Babe's philosophy was simple. He said, "Never let the fear of striking out get in your way." That's smart advice on the diamond or off.

Of course it's never wise to take foolish risks (so buckle up, slow down, and don't do anything stupid!) But when it comes to the game of life, you should not let the fear of failure keep you from taking your swings.

Success or failure can be pretty well predicted by the degree to which the heart is fully in it.

John Eldredge

In His Footsteps

Whoever serves me must follow me.
Then my servant will be with me everywhere I am.
My Father will honor anyone who serves me.

John 12:26 NCV

Jesus walks with you. Are you walking with Him? Hopefully, you will choose to walk with Him today and every day of your life.

Jesus has called upon believers of every generation (and that includes you) to follow in His footsteps. Will you follow? Please answer that question with a GREAT BIG YES. When you do, your heart will be filled with a GREAT BIG LOVE for Him!

Salvation is not a cafeteria where you take
what you want and leave the rest.
You cannot take Christ as Savior
and refuse Him as Lord.

Vance Havner

Pray for Everybody

Hatred stirs up trouble, but love forgives all wrongs.
Proverbs 10:12 NCV

It's usually pretty easy to pray for your friends and family members—all you have to do is find the time. But when it comes to praying for people who have hurt you, well that's a different matter entirely!

Like it or not, God says that you've got to pray for the folks you like and for the folks you don't like. Why? Well maybe it's because God knows that He has already forgiven you, and now He thinks it's about time for you to forgive them.

Only the truly forgiven are truly forgiving.
C. S. Lewis

It's Good for Yo

So I recommend having fun, because there is
nothing better for people to do in this world than
to eat, drink, and enjoy life. That way they will
experience some happiness along with
all the hard work God gives them.

Ecclesiastes 8:15 NLT

Sometimes, we may feel guilty about having fun when some people around the world are not having any fun at all. But God doesn't want us to spend our lives moping around with frowns on our faces. Far from it! God tells us that a happy heart is a very good thing to have.

So if you're afraid to laugh out loud, don't be. Remember that God wouldn't have given you the gift of laughter if He hadn't intended for you to use it. And remember: if you're laughing, that does not mean that you're unconcerned about people who may be hurting. It simply means that you've taken a little time to have fun, and that's good because God wants you to have a cheerful heart.

Proverbs 17:22 says that laughter is good medicine. Do yourself a favor and take that medicine whenever you can.

God Loves to Forgive

If we claim that we're free of sin, we're only fooling
ourselves. A claim like that is errant nonsense.
On the other hand, if we admit our sins—
make a clean breast of them—he won't let us down;
he'll be true to himself. He'll forgive our sins and
purge us of all wrongdoing.

1 John 1:8-9 MSG

Are you perfect? Of course not! Even if you're
a very good person, you're bound to make
mistakes and lots of them.

When you make a mistake, you must try your
best to learn from it (so that you won't make the
very same mistake again). And, if you have hurt
someone—or if you have disobeyed God—you must
ask for forgiveness. And here's the good news: when
you ask for God's forgiveness, He will always give it.
God forgives you every single time you ask Him to.
So ask!

Kid's Tip: Get busy making the world a better place.
Now that God has forgiven you, it's time for you to show
your gratitude by serving Him. (Matthew 23:11-12)

God Knows Best

However, each one must live his life in the situation
the Lord assigned when God called him.

1 Corinthians 7:17 Holman CSB

Here are three things to think about: 1. God loves you. 2. God wants what's best for you. 3. God has a plan for you.

God's plan may not always happen exactly like you want, but remember: God always knows best. Sometimes, even though you may want something very badly, you must still be patient and wait for the right time to get it. And the right time, of course, is determined by God.

Even if you don't get exactly what you want today, you can be sure that God wants what's best for you . . . today, tomorrow, and forever.

Kid's Tip: God has a plan for the world and for you. When you discover His plan for your life—and when you follow in the footsteps of His Son—you will be rewarded. The place where God is leading you is the place where you must go.

How to Treat Others

Make sure that nobody pays back wrong for wrong,
but always try to be kind to each other
and to everyone else.

1 Thessalonians 5:15 NIV

Would you like to make the world a better place? If so, you can start by practicing the Golden Rule.

Jesus said, "Whatever you want others to do for you, do also the same for them" (Mathew 7: 12 Holman CSB). That means that you should treat other people in the very same way that you want to be treated. That's the Golden Rule.

So here's what you should do: if you want to know how to treat somebody, ask the person you see every time you look into the mirror. The answer you receive will tell you exactly what to do.

Kid's Tip: How would you feel? When you're trying to decide how to treat another person, ask yourself this question: "How would I feel if somebody treated me that way?" Then, treat the other person the way that you would want to be treated.

Always Growing

When I was a child, I spoke like a child,
I thought like a child, I reasoned like a child.
When I became a man, I put aside childish things.

1 Corinthians 13:11 Holman CSB

You're growing up day by day, and it's a wonderful thing to watch. Every day, you're learning new things and doing new things. Good for you!

And when should you stop growing up? Hopefully never! That way, you'll always be learning more and doing more.

Do you think it's good to keep growing and growing and growing? If you said "yes," you're right. So remember: you're a very special person today . . . and you'll be just as special when you've grown a little bit more tomorrow.

Kid's Tip: Grown-ups still have plenty to learn . . . and so do you!

Happiness and Honesty

Lead a quiet and peaceable life in
all godliness and honesty.

1 Timothy 2:2 KJV

Have you ever said something that wasn't true?
When you did, were you sorry for what you had
said? Probably so.

When we're dishonest, we make ourselves
unhappy in surprising ways. Here are just a few
troubles that result from dishonesty: we feel guilty
and we are usually found out and we disappoint
others and we disappoint God. It's easy to see that
lies always cause more problems than they solve.

Happiness and honesty always go hand in hand.
But it's up to you to make sure that you go hand in
hand with them!

Kid's Tip: When telling the truth is hard . . . it
probably means that you're afraid of what others
might think—or what they might do—if you're
truthful. But even when telling the truth is hard, it's
always the right thing to do.

God's Angels

Don't neglect to show hospitality,
for by doing this some have welcomed angels
as guests without knowing it.

Hebrews 13:2 Holman CSB

The Bible has a lot to say about angels. But maybe you've wondered if angels are really real. If so, wonder no more! If the Bible tells you something, you can be sure that it's true.

The Bible teaches us that angels come from God, so that means they are good and they are helpful. So we don't need to fear angels . . . but neither do we need to pretend that they don't exist!

I believe in angels because the Bible
says there are angels; and I believe the Bible
to be the true Word of God.

Billy Graham

An Attitude of Kindness

Finally, all of you should be of one mind,
full of sympathy toward each other, loving one
another with tender hearts and humble minds.

1 Peter 3:8 NLT

An attitude of kindness starts in your heart and works it's way out from there.

Do you listen to your heart when it tells you to be kind to other people? Hopefully, you do. After all, lots of people in the world aren't as fortunate as you are—and some of these folks are living very near you.

Ask your parents to help you find ways to do nice things for other people. And don't forget that everybody needs love, kindness, and respect, so you should always be ready to share those things, too.

Kid's Tip: You can't just talk about it: In order to be a kind person, you must not only think kind thoughts, you must also do kind things. So get busy! The best day to become a more generous person is this day!

Listen to Directions

A fool's way is right in his own eyes, but whoever
listens to counsel is wise.

Proverbs 12:15 Holman CSB

Directions, directions, directions. It seems
like somebody is always giving you directions:
telling you where to go, how to behave, and what to
do next. But sometimes all these directions can be
confusing! How can you understand everything that
everybody tells you? The answer, of course, is that
you must pay careful attention to those directions
. . . and that means listening.

To become a careful listener, here are some
things you must do: 1. Don't talk when you're
supposed to be listening (your ears work best when
your mouth is closed); 2. Watch the person who's
giving the directions (when your eyes and ears work
together, it's easier to understand things); 3. If
you don't understand something, ask a question (it's
better to ask now than to make a mistake later).

Kid's Tip: When you listen to the things other
people have to say, it shows that you care. Listening
carefully is not just the courteous thing to do, it's
also the kind thing to do.

Make Them Proud

Give generously, for your gifts
will return to you later.

Ecclesiastes 11:1 NLT

It's tempting to be selfish, but it's wrong. It's tempting to want to keep everything for yourself, but it's better to share. It's tempting to say, "No, that's MINE!" but it's better to say, "I'll share it with you."

Are you sometimes tempted to be a little stingy? Are you sometimes tempted to say, "No, I don't want to share that!"—and then do you feel a little sorry that you said it? If that describes you, don't worry: everybody is tempted to be a little bit selfish. Your job is to remember this: even when it's tempting to be selfish, you should try very hard not to be. Because when you're generous, not selfish, you'll make your parents proud and you'll make your Father in Heaven proud, too.

Kid's Tip: Would you like to be a little happier? The Bible says that if you become a more generous person, you'll become a happier person, too.

Today's Ideas About God's Protection

Here are two important ideas. Take a few minutes to talk to your mom or dad about what these quotations mean.

Under heaven's lock and key,
we are protected by the most efficient
security system available:
the power of God.

Charles Swindoll

Prayer is our pathway not only to divine
protection, but also to a personal,
intimate relationship with God.

Shirley Dobson

God Is Close-by

Fear not, for I am with you;
Be not dismayed, for I am your God.
I will strengthen you.
Isaiah 41:10 NKJV

Here's a promise you can depend on: wherever you are, God is always there, too.

God doesn't take vacations, and He doesn't play hide-and-seek. He's always "right here, right now," waiting to hear from you. So if you're wondering where God is, wonder no more. He's here. And that's a promise!

No matter what trials we face,
Christ never leaves us.
Billy Graham

Kid's Tip: God's presence provides comfort . . . seek Him often.

You'll Feel Better About Yourself

So don't get tired of doing what is good.
Don't get discouraged and give up, for we will reap
a harvest of blessing at the appropriate time.

Galatians 6:9 NLT

The Bible teaches us to treat other people with respect, kindness, courtesy, and love. When we do, we make other people happy, we make God happy, and we feel better about ourselves, too.

So if you're wondering how to make the world—and your world—a better place, here's a great place to start: let the Golden Rule be your rule. When you do, you'll like yourself a little better . . . and so will other people.

Kid's Tip: When you treat others with respect, you will feel better about yourself.

Today's Happiness

But happy are those . . .
whose hope is in the LORD their God.
Psalm 146:5 NLT

If we could decide to be happy "once and for all,"
life would be so much simpler, but it doesn't
seem to work that way. If we want happiness to last,
we need to create good thoughts every day that we
live. Yesterday's good thoughts don't count . . . we've
got to think more good thoughts today.

Each new day is a gift from God, so treat it
that way. Think about it like this: today is another
wonderful chance to celebrate God's gifts.

So celebrate—starting now—and keep
celebrating forever!

Kid's Tip: Better self-control can help make
you happy: the better you behave, the more fun
you'll have. And don't let anybody try to tell you
otherwise.

An Honest Heart

In every way be an example of doing good deeds.
When you teach, do it with honesty and seriousness.

Titus 2:7 NCV

Where does honesty begin? In your own heart and your own head. If you sincerely want to be an honest person, then you must ask God to help you find the courage and the determination to be honest all of the time.

Honesty is not a "sometimes" thing. If you intend to be a truthful person, you must make truthfulness a habit that becomes so much a part of you that you don't have to decide whether or not you're going to tell the truth. Instead, you will simply tell the truth because it's the kind of person you are.

Lying is an easy habit to fall into, and a terrible one. So make up your mind that you're going to be an honest person, and then stick to your decision. That's what your parents want you to do, and that's what God wants, too. And since they love you more than you know, trust them. And always tell the truth.

Kindness Starts with You

Be kind to one another, tender-hearted,
forgiving each other, just as God in Christ
also has forgiven you.

Ephesians 4:32 NASB

If you're waiting for other people to be nice to
you before you're nice to them, you've got it
backwards. Kindness starts with you! You see, you
can never control what other people will say or do,
but you can control your own behavior.

The Bible tells us that we should never stop
doing good deeds as long as we live. Kindness is God's
way, and it should be our way, too.

Kid's Tip: Kind is as kind does: In order to be a
kind person, you must do kind things. Thinking about
them isn't enough. So get busy! Your family and
friends need all the kindness they can get!

Love Your Family

Love must be without hypocrisy. Detest evil;
cling to what is good. Show family affection to
one another with brotherly love.
Outdo one another in showing honor.

Romans 12:9-10 Holman CSB

Your family is a wonderful, one-of-a-kind gift from God. And your family members love you very much—what a blessing it is to be loved!

Have you ever really stopped to think about how much you are loved? Your parents love you (of course) and so does everybody else in your family. But it doesn't stop there. You're also an important part of God's family . . . and He loves you more than you can imagine.

What should you do about all the love that comes your way? You should accept it; you should be thankful for it; and you should share it . . . starting now!

I like to think of my family as a big, beautiful patchwork quilt—each of us so different yet stitched together by love and life experiences.

Barbara Johnson

Everybody Makes Mistakes

Instead, God has chosen the world's foolish things
to shame the wise, and God has chosen
the world's weak things to shame the strong.

1 Corinthians 1:27 Holman CSB

Do you make mistakes? Of course you do . . .
everybody does. When you make a mistake, you
must try your best to learn from it so that you won't
make the very same mistake again. And, if you have
hurt someone—or if you have disobeyed God—you
must ask for forgiveness.

Remember: mistakes are a part of life, but the
biggest mistake you can make is to keep making the
same mistake over and over and over again.

Kid's Tip: Fix it sooner rather than later: If you
make a mistake, the time to make things better is
now, not later! The sooner you admit your mistake,
the better.

Obeying God

But be doers of the word and not hearers only.

James 1:22 Holman CSB

How can you show God how much you love Him? By obeying His commandments, that's how! When you follow God's rules, you show Him that you have real respect for Him and for His Son.

Sometimes, you will be tempted to disobey God, but don't do it. And sometimes you'll be tempted to disobey your parents or your teachers . . . but don't do that, either.

When your parent steps away or a teacher looks away, it's up to you to control yourself. And of this you can be sure: If you really want to control yourself, you can do it!

Kid's Tip: Associate with friends who, by their words and actions, encourage you to obey God.

Don't Copy Friends Who Misbehave

Stay away from a foolish man; you will gain
no knowledge from his speech.

Proverbs 14:7 Holman CSB

If your friends misbehave, do you misbehave right along with them, or do you tell them to stop? Usually, it's much easier to go along with your friends, even if you know they're misbehaving. But it's always better to do the right thing, even if it's hard.

Sometimes, grownups must stand up for the things they believe in. When they do, it can be hard for them, too. But the Bible tells us over and over again that we should do the right thing, not the easy thing.

When your friends misbehave, it can spoil everything. So if your friends behave badly, don't copy them! And if your friends keep behaving badly, choose different friends.

Comparison is the root of all feelings of inferiority.

James Dobson

Becoming a More Patient Person

Be gentle to all, able to teach, patient.
2 Timothy 2:24 NKJV

The Book of Proverbs tells us that patience is a very good thing. But for most of us, patience can also be a very hard thing. After all, we have many things that we want, and we want them NOW! But the Bible tells us that we must learn to wait patiently for the things that God has in store for us.

Are you having trouble being patient? If so, remember that patience takes practice, and lots of it, so keep trying. And if you make a mistake, don't be too upset. After all, if you're going to be a really patient person, you shouldn't just be patient with others, you should also be patient with yourself.

Kid's Tip: An important part of growing up is learning to be patient with others and with yourself. And one more thing: learn from everybody's mistakes, especially your own.

Learning to Control Yourself

But endurance must do its complete work,
so that you may be mature and complete,
lacking nothing.

James 1:4 Holman CSB

If you're having trouble learning how to control your actions or your emotions, you're not alone! Most people have problems with self-control from time to time, so don't be discouraged. Just remember that self-control requires practice and lots of it. So if you're a little discouraged, don't give up. Just keep working on improving your self-control until you get better at it. . . . and if you keep trying, you can be sure that sooner or later, you will get better at it.

Kid's Tip: The world encourages instant gratification but God's Work takes time. Remember the words of C. H. Spurgeon: "By perseverance, the snail reached the ark."

Today's Ideas About
What Happens When You Pray

Here are two important ideas. Take a few minutes to talk to your mom or dad about what these quotations mean.

Prayer accomplishes more than anything else.
Bill Bright

Prayer succeeds when all else fails.
E. M. Bounds

Be Respectful

Show respect for all people.
Love the brothers and sisters of God's family.
1 Peter 2:17 ICB

*A*re you polite and respectful to your parents and teachers? And do you do your best to treat everybody with the respect they deserve? If you want to obey God's rules, then you should be able to answer yes to these questions.

Remember this: the Bible teaches you to be a respectful person—and if it's right there in the Bible, it's certainly the right thing to do!

Kid's Tip: Calm down . . . sooner rather than later! If you're angry with your mom or your dad, don't blurt out something unkind. If you can't say anything nice, go to your room and don't come out until you can.

Slow Down!

Knowing God leads to self-control.
Self-control leads to patient endurance,
and patient endurance leads to godliness.

2 Peter 1:6 NLT

Maybe you're one of those people who tries to do everything fast, faster, or fastest! If so, maybe you sometimes do things before you think about the consequences of your actions. If that's the case, it's probably a good idea to slow down a little bit so you can think before you act. When you do, you'll soon discover the value of thinking carefully about things before you get started. And while you're at it, it's probably a good idea to think before you speak, too. After all, you'll never have to apologize for something that you didn't say.

Discipline is training that develops and corrects.

Charles Stanley

Sharing

If you have two shirts, share with the person
who does not have one.
If you have food, share that too.

Luke 3:11 ICB

How many times have you heard someone say, "Don't touch that; it's mine!" If you're like most of us, you've heard those words many times and you may have even said them yourself.

The Bible tells us that it's better for us to share things than it is to keep them all to ourselves. And the Bible also tells us that when we share, it's best to do so cheerfully. So today and every day, let's share. It's the best way because it's God's way.

Kid's Tip: Your acts of kindness and generosity will speak far louder than words.

The Words You Speak

If anyone considers himself religious and yet does
not keep a tight rein on his tongue, he deceives
himself and his religion is worthless.

James 1:26 NIV

The words you speak are important. If you speak
kind words, you make other people feel better.
And that's exactly what you should do!

How hard is it to say a kind word? Not very!
Yet sometimes we're so busy that we forget to say
the very things that might make other people feel
better.

Kind words help; cruel words hurt. It's as
simple as that. And, when we say the right thing
at the right time, we give a gift that can change
somebody's day or somebody's life.

Kid's Tip: If you're not sure that it's the right thing
to say, don't say it! And if you're not sure that it's
the truth, don't tell it.

Try to Memorize This Verse

This is the day the LORD has made;
let us rejoice and be glad in it.
Psalm 118:24 NIV

This is an important Bible verse.
Practice saying it several times. And then, talk to
mom or dad about exactly what the verse means . . .

A Tip for Parents: Talk to your child about . . .

The need to celebrate life today
and every day.

Everlasting Protection

The Lord is my rock, my fortress, and my deliverer,
my God, my mountain where I seek refuge.
My shield, the horn of my salvation, my stronghold,
my refuge, and my Savior.

2 Samuel 22:2-3 Holman CSB

Life isn't always easy. Far from it! Sometimes, life can be very hard indeed. But even when we're upset or hurt, we must remember that we're protected by a loving Heavenly Father.

When we're worried, God can reassure us; when we're sad, God can comfort us. When our feelings are hurt, God is not just near, He is here. We must lift our thoughts and prayers to our Father in heaven. When we do, He will answer our prayers. Why? Because He is our shepherd, and He has promised to protect us now and forever.

Kid's Tip: Your only real security comes from the loving heart of God—and from the salvation that flows from His only begotten Son.

No More Tantrums

A patient person [shows] great understanding,
but a quick-tempered one promotes foolishness.

Proverbs 14:29 Holman CSB

Temper tantrums are so silly. And so is pouting. So, of course, is whining. When we lose our tempers, we say things that we shouldn't say, and we do things that we shouldn't do. Too bad!

The Bible tells us that it is foolish to become angry and that it is wise to remain calm. That's why we should learn to control our tempers before our tempers control us.

Kid's Tip: No more tantrums! If you think you're about to pitch a fit or throw a tantrum, slow down, catch your breath, and walk away if you must. It's better to walk away—and keep walking—than it is to blurt out angry words that can't be un-blurted.

Right and Wrong

Lead a tranquil and quiet life
in all godliness and dignity.
1 Timothy 2:2 Holman CSB

If you're old enough to know right from wrong, then you're old enough to do something about it. In other words, you should always try to do the right thing, and you should also do your very best not to do the wrong thing.

The more self-control you have, the easier it is to do the right thing. Why? Because, when you learn to think first and do things next, you avoid lots of silly mistakes. So here's great advice: first, slow down long enough to figure out the right thing to do—and then do it. You'll make yourself happy, and you'll make lots of other people happy, too.

Kid's Tip: Good behavior leads to a happy life. And bad behavior doesn't. Behave accordingly.

Blessed to Be a Blessing

God has given gifts to each of you from his great
variety of spiritual gifts. Manage them well
so that God's generosity can flow through you.

1 Peter 4:10 NLT

Jesus said, "It is more blessed to give than
to receive." That means that we should be
generous with other people—but sometimes we don't
feel much like sharing. Instead of sharing the things
that we have, we want to keep them all to ourselves.
That's when we must remember that God doesn't
want selfishness to rule our hearts; He wants us to
be generous.

Are you lucky enough to have nice things? If so,
God's instructions are clear: you must share your
blessings with others. And that's exactly the way
it should be. After all, think how generous God has
been with you.

Kid's Tip: Too many toys? Give them away! Are you
one of those lucky kids who has more toys that you
can play with? If so, remember that not everyone is
so lucky. Ask your parents to help you give some of
your toys to kids who need them more than you do.

Listen to God

Continue to ask, and God will give to you.
Continue to search, and you will find.
Continue to knock, and the door will open for you.

Matthew 7:7 ICB

God has many things he wants to tell us. And for starters, He wants us to be loving, kind, and patient, not rude or mean!

The Bible tells us that God is love and that if we wish to know Him, we must have love in our hearts. Sometimes, of course, when we're tired, angry, or frustrated, it is very hard for us to be loving. Thankfully, anger and frustration are feelings that come and go, but God's love lasts forever.

If you'd like to become a more patient person, talk to God in prayer, listen to what He says, and share His love with your family and friends. God is always listening, and He's ready to talk to you . . . now!

Kid's Tip: If you want more from life, ask more from God (and keep asking Him) until He answers your prayers.

Try to Memorize This Verse

A cheerful heart brings a smile
to your face; a sad heart
makes it hard to get through the day.
Proverbs 15:13 MSG

This is an important Bible verse.
Practice saying it several times. And then, talk to
mom or dad about exactly what the verse means . . .

A Tip for Parents: Talk to your child about . . .

The benefits of a happy heart.

Golden Rule

Do for other people the same things
you want them to do for you.

Matthew 7:12 ICB

Some rules are easier to understand than they are to live by. Jesus told us that we should treat other people in the same way that we would want to be treated: that's the Golden Rule. But sometimes, especially when we're tired or upset, that rule is very hard to follow.

Jesus wants us to treat other people with respect, kindness, courtesy, and love. When we do, we make our families and friends happy . . . and we make our Father in heaven very proud.

Kid's Tip: How would you feel? When you're trying to decide how to treat another person, ask yourself this question: "How would I feel if somebody treated me that way?" Then, treat the other person the way that you would want to be treated.

The Wonder of Heaven

Be glad and rejoice,
because your reward is great in heaven.
Matthew 5:12 Holman CSB

The Bible makes this important promise: when you give your heart to Jesus, you will live forever with Him in heaven. And Jesus told us that His house has "many mansions" (John 14:1-3).

Even though we don't know everything about heaven, we do know this: heaven will be a wonderful place, a place of joy and wonder, a place where we will be reunited with our loved ones and with God. It's wonderful to think about . . . and a priceless gift from God.

The main joy of heaven will be the heavenly Father greeting us in a time and place of rejoicing, celebration, joy, and great reunion.
Bill Bright

Today's Ideas About
Serving Other People

Here are two important ideas. Take a few minutes to talk to your mom or dad about what these quotations mean.

God will open up places of service for
you as He sees you are ready.
Meanwhile, study the Bible
and give yourself a chance to grow.

Warren Wiersbe

Carve your name on hearts,
not on marble.

C. H. Spurgeon

Joyful Abundance

Shout with joy to the LORD, O earth!
Worship the LORD with gladness.
Come before him, singing with joy.

Psalm 100:1-2 NLT

Have you made the choice to rejoice? Hopefully so. After all, if you're a Christian, you have plenty of reasons to be joyful.

So today, think about this: God has given you too many blessings to count, but you can certainly count some of those blessings. Your job is to honor God with your prayers, your words, your behavior, and your joy.

According to Jesus, it is God's will that
His children be filled with the joy of life.

Catherine Marshall

The Best Time to Praise God

The LORD is my strength and song,
and He has become my salvation; He is my God,
and I will praise Him.

Exodus 15:2 NIV

When is the best time to praise God? In church? Before dinner is served? When we tuck little children into bed? None of the above. The best time to praise God is all day, every day, to the greatest extent we can, with thanksgiving in our hearts, and with a song on our lips. Dr. Wayne Oates once admitted, "Many of my prayers are made with my eyes open. You see, it seems I'm always praying about something, and it's not always convenient—or safe—to close my eyes." Dr. Oates understood that God always hears our prayers and that the position of our eyelids is of no concern to Him.

Today, find a little more time to lift your concerns to God in prayer, and praise Him for all that He has done. Whether your eyes are open or closed, He's listening.

Kid's Tip: Make it a habit to praise God many times each day, beginning with morning devotionals.

Don't Tell Lies

Therefore laying aside falsehood, speak truth,
each one of you, with his neighbor,
for we are members of one another.

Ephesians 4:25 NASB

Sometimes people lie, and sometimes they get away with it. But that doesn't mean that it's wise to lie. And that doesn't make lying the right thing to do. Far from it.

Whatever the problem, lying is always a bad solution. And, besides, lying is always against the will of God. So even if other people lie, don't ever believe that they have lied successfully. There's no such thing as a successful lie.

When you talk, choose the very same words
that you would use if Jesus were looking
over your shoulder. Because He is.

Marie T. Freeman

Forgive Other People's Mistakes

I will instruct you and teach you in the way you should go; I will counsel you and watch over you.

Psalm 32:8 NIV

When other people make mistakes, you must find a way to forgive them. And when you make mistakes, as you will from time to time, you must hope that other people will forgive you, too.

When you have done things that you regret, you should apologize, you should clean up the mess you've made, you should learn from your mistakes, and—last but not least—you should forgive yourself. Mistakes happen . . . it's simply a fact of life, and it's simply a part of growing up. So don't be too hard on yourself, especially if you've learned something along the way.

Father, take our mistakes and turn them into opportunities.

Max Lucado

Keep Your Eye upon the Donut

I can do everything through him
that gives me strength.

Philippians 4:13 NIV

Here's a poem that was seen many years ago in a
small donut shop:

As you travel through life brother,
Whatever be your goal,
Keep your eye upon the donut,
And not upon the hole.

What do you think these words mean? Well, this
little poem can teach you an important lesson: You
should spend more time looking at the things you
have, not worrying about the things you don't have.

When you think about it, you've got more
blessings than you can count. So make it a habit to
thank God for the gifts He's given you, and don't
feel jealous, angry, or sad about all the other stuff.

Kid's Tip: Your attitude toward the future will help
create your future.

Patience Please!

I wait for the Lord; I wait,
and put my hope in His word.

Psalm 130:5 Holman CSB

God has a perfect idea of the kind of people He wants us to become. And for starters, He wants us to be loving, kind, and patient—not rude or mean!

The Bible tells us that God is love and that if we wish to know Him, we must have love in our hearts. Sometimes, of course, when we're tired, angry, or frustrated, it is very hard for us to be loving. Thankfully, anger and frustration are feelings that come and go, but God's love lasts forever.

If you'd like to become a more patient person, talk to God in prayer, listen to what He says, and share His love with your family and friends. God is always listening, and He's ready to talk to you . . . now!

Kid's Tip: God has been patient with you . . . now it's your turn to be patient with others.

Know When to Say No

Wisdom will save you from the ways
of wicked men . . . .
Proverbs 2:12 NIV

It happens to all of us at one time or another: a friend asks us to do something that we think is wrong. What should we do? Should we try to please our friend by doing something bad? No way! It's not worth it!

Trying to please our friends is okay. What's not okay is misbehaving in order to do so. Do you have a friend who encourages you to misbehave? Hopefully you don't have any friends like that. But if you do, say "No, NO, NOOOOOO!" And what if your friend threatens to break up the friendship? Let him! Friendships like that just aren't worth it.

You will get untold flak for prioritizing God's revealed and present will for your life over man's . . . but, boy, is it worth it.
Beth Moore

Today's Ideas About
Cheerfulness

Here are two important ideas. Take a few minutes to talk to your mom or dad about what these quotations mean.

When we bring sunshine into the lives of others, we're warmed by it ourselves. When we spill a little happiness, it splashes on us.

Barbara Johnson

We may run, walk, stumble, drive, or fly, but let us never lose sight of the reason for the journey, or miss a chance to see a rainbow on the way.

Gloria Gaither

He Answers

. . . I know the thoughts that I think toward you,
says the Lord, thoughts of peace and not of evil,
to give you a future and a hope. Then you will
call upon Me and go and pray to Me,
and I will listen to you.
Jeremiah 29:11-12 NKJV

In case you've been wondering, wonder no more—God does answer your prayers. What God does not do is this: He does not always answer your prayers as soon as you might like, and He does not always answer your prayers by saying "Yes."

God answers prayers not only according to our wishes but also according to His master plan. And guess what? We don't know that plan . . . but we can know the Planner.

Are you praying? Then you can be sure that God is listening. And sometime soon, He'll answer!

You don't need fancy words or religious phrases.
Just tell God the way it really is.
Jim Cymbala

Respect for Others

Being respected is more important
than having great riches.

Proverbs 22:1 ICB

Do you try to have a respectful attitude towards everybody? Hopefully so!

Should you be respectful of grown ups? Of course. Teachers? Certainly. Family members? Yes. Friends? Yep, but it doesn't stop there. The Bible teaches us to treat all people with respect.

Respect for others is habit-forming: the more you do it, the easier it becomes. So start practicing right now. Say lots of kind words and do lots of kind things, because when it comes to kindness and respect, practice makes perfect.

Kid's Tip: "The least of these . . . ": How did Jesus treat the people who lived on the edges of society? With patience, respect, and love.

When Nobody Is Watching

Moderation is better than muscle,
self-control better than political power.

Proverbs 16:32 MSG

When your teachers or parents aren't watching, what should you do? The answer, of course, is that you should behave exactly like you would if they were watching you. But sometimes, you may be tempted to do otherwise.

When a parent steps away or a teacher looks away, you may be tempted to say something or do something that you would not do if they were standing right beside you. But remember this: when nobody's watching, it's up to you to control yourself. And that's exactly what everybody wants you to do: your teachers want you to control yourself, and so do your parents. And so, by the way, does God.

God nowhere tells us to give up things for the sake of giving them up. He tells us to give them up for the sake of the only thing worth having—
life with Himself.

Oswald Chambers

God Wants You to Share

I will make you into a great nation and I will bless
you; I will make your name great, and you will be
a blessing. I will bless those who bless you,
and whoever curses you I will curse; and all peoples
on earth will be blessed through you.

Genesis 12:2-3 NIV

You've heard it plenty of times from your
parents and teachers: share your things. But
it's important to realize that sharing isn't just
something that grown-ups want you to do. It's also
something that God wants you to do, too.

The word "possessions" is another way of
describing the stuff that belongs to you: your
clothes, your toys, your books, and things like that
are "your possessions."

Jesus says that you should learn how to share
your possessions without feeling bad about it.
Sometimes, of course, it's very hard to share and
very easy to be stingy. But God wants you to share—
and to keep sharing! Since that's what God wants,
it's what you should want, too.

God's Friendship

Greater love has no one than this,
that he lay down his life for his friends.
John 15:13 NIV

There's an old song that says, "What a friend we have in Jesus." Those words are certainly true! When you invite Him into your heart, Jesus will be your friend forever. If you make mistakes, He'll still be your friend. If you behave badly, He'll still love you. If you feel sorry or sad, He can help you feel better if you ask Him to.

Jesus wants you to have a happy, healthy life. He wants you to behave yourself, and He wants you to take care of yourself. And now, it's up to you to do your best to live up to the hopes and dreams of your very best friend: Jesus.

Kid's Tip: Jesus loves you, this you know . . . and they should too! Of course you know that Jesus loves you. But it's up to you to make sure that they know that you know. So remind them often.

You're Not Expected to Be Perfect

If we confess our sins to him,
he is faithful and just to forgive us
and to cleanse us from every wrong.

1 John 1:9 NLT

When you make a mistake, do you get really mad at yourself . . . or maybe really, really, really mad? Hopefully not! After all, everybody makes mistakes, and nobody is expected to be perfect.

Even when you make mistakes, God loves you . . . so you should love yourself, too.

So the next time you make a mistake, learn from it. And after you've learned your lesson, try never to make that same mistake again. But don't be too hard on yourself. God doesn't expect you to be perfect, and since He loves you anyway, you should feel that way, too.

Kid's Tip: A mistake is never permanent (unless you do nothing to fix it).

Stuff, Things, and More Stuff

Don't be obsessed with getting more material
things. Be relaxed with what you have.

Hebrews 13:5 MSG

Here's something to remember about stuff: It's
not that important!

Lots of people are in love with money and the
things that money can buy. God is not. God cares
about people, not possessions, and so must you.

You should not be too concerned about the
clothes you wear, or the things you own. And above
all, don't ever let your self-esteem depend upon the
things that you (or your parents) own.

The stuff that you own isn't nearly as important
as the love that you feel in your heart—love for
your family, love for your friends, and love for your
Father in heaven.

Kid's Tip: Your possessions are actually God's
possessions, so try to use them for His purposes.

It's a Good Feeling to Obey and Forgive

This is love for God: to obey his commands.

1 John 5:3 NIV

We know that it's right to forgive other people and wrong to stay angry with them. But sometimes, it's so much easier to do the wrong thing than it is to do the right thing, especially when we're tired or frustrated.

When you do the right thing by forgiving other people, you'll feel good because you'll know that you're obeying God. And that's a very good feeling indeed. So make this promise to yourself and keep it: play by the rules—God's rules. You'll always be glad you did.

Kid's Tip: Your obedience to God is a demonstration of the gratitude that you feel in your heart for the blessings you have been given.

Today's Ideas About
Not Giving Up

Here are two important ideas. Take a few minutes to talk to your mom or dad about what these quotations mean.

By perseverance the snail reached the ark.

C. H. Spurgeon

Battles are won in the trenches, in the grit and grime of courageous determination; they are won day by day in the arena of life.

Charles Swindoll

Lost in the Crowd?

We must obey God rather than men.

Acts 5:29 Holman CSB

Rick Warren observed, "Those who follow the crowd usually get lost in it." We know those words to be true, but oftentimes we fail to live by them. Instead of trusting God for guidance, we imitate our friends and suffer the consequences.

Instead of getting lost in the crowd, you should find guidance from your parents and from God. When you do, you'll be happier . . . much happier!

Obey God one step at a time,
then the next step will come into view.

Catherine Marshall

Kid's Tip: Being obedient to God means that you cannot always please other people . . .

Be Patient

You must do this not only while they are watching
you, to please them. With all your heart you must do
what God wants as people who are obeying Christ.
Do your work with enthusiasm. Work as if
you were serving the Lord, not as if you were
serving only men and women.

Ephesians 6:6-7 NCV

If you've lost patience with someone, or if you're
angry, take a deep breath and then ask yourself
a simple question: "How would Jesus behave if He
were here?" The answer to that question will tell
you what to do.

Jesus was quick to speak kind words, and He was
quick to forgive others. We must do our best to
be like Him. When we do, we will be patient, loving,
understanding, and kind.

We have in Jesus Christ a perfect example of
how to put God's truth into practice.

Bill Bright

It Pays to Praise

Is anyone happy? Let him sing songs of praise.

James 5:13 NIV

The Bible makes it clear: it pays to say "thank You" to God. But sometimes, we may not feel like thanking anybody, not even our Father in heaven.

If we ever stop praising God, it's a big mistake . . . a VERY BIG mistake.

When you stop to think about it, God has been very generous with you . . . and He deserves a great big "thanks" for all those amazing gifts.

Do you want an attitude that pleases God? Then make sure that your attitude praises God. And don't just praise Him on Sunday morning. Praise Him every day, starting with this one.

Kid's Tip: When you pray, don't just ask God for things; also praise Him.

Day 110

Try to Memorize This Verse

Jesus answered and said to him,
"Truly, truly, I say to you,
unless one is born again
he cannot see the kingdom of God."
John 3:3 NASB

This is an important Bible verse.
Practice saying it several times. And then, talk to
mom or dad about exactly what the verse means . . .

A Tip for Parents: Talk to your child about . . .

The need to be born again

Keep Learning About Self-Control

For the Son of man shall come in the glory of his Father with his angels; and then he shall reward every man according to his works.

Matthew 16:27 KJV

Who needs to learn more about self-control? You do! Why? Well, for one thing, you'll discover that good things happen to people (like you) who are wise enough to think ahead and smart enough to look before they leap.

Whether you're at home or at school, you'll learn that the best rewards go to the kids who control their behavior—not to the people who let their behaviors control them!

The problem is that we want the rewards of success without paying the price.

John Maxwell

Look Ahead

Learn the truth and never reject it.
Get wisdom, self-control, and understanding.
Proverbs 23:23 NCV

Maybe you've heard this old saying: "Look before you leap." What does that saying mean? It means that you should stop and think before you do something. Otherwise, you might be sorry you did it.

Your parents are trying to teach you how to slow down and make better decisions. Why? Because your parents want what's best for you, that's why!

So here's something that you can do: think about the consequences of your behaviors before you do something silly . . . or dangerous . . . or both.

Kid's Tip: When you learn how to control yourself, you'll be happier . . . and your parents will be happier, too.

Start Sharing Now

Never walk away from someone who deserves help;
your hand is God's hand for that person.

Proverbs 3:27 MSG

When is the best time to share? Whenever you can—and that means right now, if possible. When you start thinking about the things you can share, you probably think mostly about things that belong to you (like toys or clothes), but there are many more things you can share (like love, kindness, encouragement, and prayers). That means you have the opportunity to share something with somebody almost any time you want. And that's exactly what God wants you to do—so start sharing now and don't ever stop.

It is the duty of every Christian to be
Christ to his neighbor.

Martin Luther

Today's Ideas About Perfectionism

Here are two important ideas. Take a few minutes to talk to your mom or dad about what these quotations mean.

What makes a Christian a Christian is not perfection but forgiveness.

Max Lucado

The happiest people in the world are not those who have no problems, but the people who have learned to live with those things that are less than perfect.

James Dobson

Count Your Blessings

Enter his gates with thanksgiving; go into his courts
with praise. Give thanks to him and bless his name.
For the Lord is good. His unfailing love continues
forever, and his faithfulness continues
to each generation.

Psalm 100:4-5 NLT

If you sat down and began counting your blessings,
how long would it take? A very, very long time!
Your blessings include your life, your family, your
friends, your talents, and possessions, for starters.
But, your greatest blessing—a gift that is yours
for the asking—is God's gift of eternal life through
Christ Jesus.

You can never count up every single blessing that
God has given you, but it doesn't hurt to try . . . so
get ready, get set, go—start counting your blessings
RIGHT NOW!

Kid's Tip: There is value in thanking God for His
perfect plan even when you don't understand that
plan.

Try to Memorize This Verse

The Lord is my light and my salvation;
whom shall I fear?
The Lord is the strength of my life;
of whom shall I be afraid?

Psalm 27:1 KJV

This is an important Bible verse.
Practice saying it several times. And then, talk to
mom or dad about exactly what the verse means . . .

A Tip for Parents: Talk to your child about . . .

The courage God provides

Following Jesus

And he saith unto them, follow me,
and I will make you fishers of men.
And they straightway left their nets,
and followed him.

Matthew 4:19-20 KJV

If Jesus were here, how would He behave? He would be loving and forgiving. He would worship God with sincere devotion. He would serve other people, and he would always abide by the Golden Rule. If Jesus were here, He would stand up for truth and speak out against evil.

We read in the Bible that Jesus wants each of us to do our best to be like Him. We can't be perfect Christians, but we can do our best to obey God's commandments and to follow Christ's example. When we do so, we bring honor to the One who gave His life for each of us.

Kid's Tip: When you have an important decision to make, stop for a minute and think about how Jesus would behave if He were in your shoes.

A Pleasing Attitude

Set your minds on what is above,
not on what is on the earth.

Colossians 3:2 Holman CSB

God knows everything about you, including your attitude. And when your attitude is good, God is pleased . . . very pleased.

Are you interested in pleasing God? Are you interested in pleasing your parents? Your teachers? And your friends? If so, try to make your attitude the best it can be. When you try hard to have a good attitude, you'll make other people feel better—and you'll make yourself feel better, too.

Kid's Tip: A Happy Heart Every Day: Remember that you can choose to have a good attitude or a not-so good attitude. And it's a choice you make every day.

Your Most Important Book

But grow in the grace and knowledge of our Lord
and Savior Jesus Christ. To Him be the glory
both now and forever. Amen.

2 Peter 3:18 NKJV

What book contains everything that God has to say about His rules and His Son? The Bible, of course. If you read the Bible every day, you'll soon learn how God wants you to behave.

Since doing the right thing (and the smart thing) is important to God, it should be important to you, too. And you'll learn what's right by reading the Bible.

The Bible is the most important book you'll ever own. It's God's Holy Word. Read it every day, and follow its instructions. When you do, you'll be safe now and forever.

Kid's Tip: Read the Bible? Every Day!: try to read your Bible with your parents every day. If they forget, remind them!

A Continual Feast?

A cheerful heart has a continual feast.
Proverbs 15:15 Holman CSB

What is a continual feast? It's a little bit like a non-stop birthday party: fun, fun, and more fun! The Bible tells us that a cheerful heart can make life like a continual feast, and that's something worth working for.

Where does cheerfulness begin? It begins inside each of us; it begins in the heart. So today and every day, let's be thankful to God for His blessings, and let's show our thanks by sharing good cheer wherever we go. This old world needs all the cheering up it can get . . . and so do we!

When we bring sunshine into the lives of others,
we're warmed by it ourselves. When we spill
a little happiness, it splashes on us.

Barbara Johnson

Getting to Know God

Stay clear of silly stories that get dressed up
as religion. Exercise daily in God—
no spiritual flabbiness, please!

1 Timothy 4:7 MSG

Want to know God better? Then schedule a
meeting with Him every day.

Each day has 1,440 minutes—will you spend a
few of those minutes with your Heavenly Father?
He deserves that much of your time and more. God
wants you to pay attention to Him. So, if you haven't
already done so, form the habit of spending quality
time with your Creator. He deserves it . . . and so,
for that matter, do you.

Kid's Tip: Do you have a special place where you
and your parents read daily devotionals? If not, you
should ask your mom or dad to help you think of a
good place where the two of you can read the Bible
and talk to God.

Tell It Like It Is

I have no greater joy than this: to hear
that my children are walking in the truth.
3 John 1:4 Holman CSB

Perhaps you've heard the story of the boy who cried "wolf!" In that story, the boy exaggerated his problems and eventually got himself into BIG trouble!

When we pretend that our troubles are worse than they really are, we may earn a little sympathy now, but we'll invite lots of trouble later.

If you're ever tempted to cry "wolf!", don't. Exaggeration wasn't good for the boy who cried "wolf!", and it's not good for you.

Kid's Tip: Don't Exaggerate! All of us have enough troubles without pretending that we have more.

Try to Memorize This Verse

He will wipe away every tear
from their eyes.
Death will exist no longer;
grief, crying, and pain will exist
no longer, because the previous things
have passed away.

Revelation 21:4 Holman CSB

This is an important Bible verse.
Practice saying it several times. And then, talk to
mom or dad about exactly what the verse means . . .

A Tip for Parents: Talk to your child about . . .

Heaven

Do Yourself a Favor

And whenever you stand praying,
if you have anything against anyone, forgive him,
so that your Father in heaven may also
forgive you your wrongdoing.

Mark 11:25 Holman CSB

When you forgive somebody else, you're actually doing yourself a favor. Why? Because when you forgive the other person, you get rid of angry feelings that can make you unhappy.

Are you still angry about something that happened yesterday, or the day before that, or the day before that? Do yourself a big favor: forgive everybody (including yourself, if necessary). When you do, you won't change what happened yesterday, but you will make today a whole lot better.

Kid's Tip: If you're having trouble forgiving someone else . . . think how many times other people have forgiven you!

Love That Lasts

It is good and pleasant when God's people
live together in peace!
Psalm 133:1 NCV

*A*re your friends kind to you? And are your
friends nice to other people, too? If so,
congratulations! If not, it's probably time to start
looking for a few new friends. After all, it's really
not very much fun to be around people who aren't
nice to everybody.

The Bible teaches that a pure heart is a
wonderful blessing. It's up to each of us to fill our
hearts with love for God, love for Jesus, and love
for all people. When we do, we feel better about
ourselves.

Do you want to be the best person you can be?
Then invite the love of Christ into your heart and
share His love with your family and friends. And
remember that lasting love always comes from a
pure heart . . . like yours!

Kid's Tip: The Best Rule for Making and Keeping
Friends . . . is the Golden one.

Gentle Words

Always be humble, gentle, and patient,
accepting each other in love.

Ephesians 4:2 NCV

The Bible tells us that gentle words are helpful and that cruel words are not. But sometimes, especially when we're angry or frustrated, our words and our actions may not be so gentle. Sometimes, we may say things or do things that are unkind or hurtful to others. When we do, we're wrong.

So the next time you're tempted to strike out in anger, don't. And if you want to help your family and friends, remember that gentle words are better than harsh words and good deeds are better than the other kind. Always!

I choose gentleness. Nothing is won by force.
I choose to be gentle. If I raise my voice may
it be only in praise. If I clench my fist, may it be
only in prayer. If I make a demand,
may it be only of myself.

Max Lucado

God's Promise of Love

His banner over me was love.

Song of Solomon 2:4 KJV

In the Bible, God makes this amazing promise—He promises that He loves you.

And it's a promise that He intends to keep.

No matter where you are (and no matter what you've done), you're never beyond the reach of God's love. So take time today (and every day) to thank Him for love that is too big to understand with your head, but not too big to feel with your heart.

The life of faith is a daily exploration of the constant and countless ways in which God's grace and love are experienced.

Eugene Peterson

God loves you and wants you to experience peace and life—abundant and eternal.

Billy Graham

Today's Ideas About
Patience

Here are two important ideas. Take a few minutes
to talk to your mom or dad about what these
quotations mean.

In the Bible, patience is not a passive
acceptance of circumstances.
It is a courageous perseverance
in the face of suffering and difficulty.
Warren Wiersbe

We must learn to wait.
There is grace supplied to the one
who waits.
Mrs. Charles E. Cowman

Obeying God and Happy

I will praise you, Lord, with all my heart.
I will tell all the miracles you have done.
I will be happy because of you; God Most High,
I will sing praises to your name.

Psalm 9:1-2 NCV

Do you want to be happy? Here are some things you should do: Love God and His Son, Jesus; obey the Golden Rule; and always try to do the right thing. When you do these things, you'll discover that happiness goes hand-in-hand with good behavior.

The happiest people do not misbehave; the happiest people are not cruel or greedy. The happiest people don't say unkind things. The happiest people are those who love God and follow his rules—starting, of course, with the Golden one.

Kid's Tip: Sometimes happy, sometimes not: Even if you're a very good person, you shouldn't expect to be happy all the time. Sometimes, things will happen to make you sad, and it's okay to be sad when bad things happen to you or to your friends and family. But remember: through good times and bad, you'll always be happier if you obey the rules of your Father in heaven. So obey them!

God Knows My Heart

Create in me a pure heart, God,
and make my spirit right again.

Psalm 51:10 NCV

Other people see you from the outside. God sees you from the inside—God sees your heart.

Kindness comes from the heart. So does sharing. So if you want to show your family and your friends that your heart is filled with kindness and love, one way to do it is by sharing. But don't worry about trying to show God what kind of person you are. He already knows your heart, and He loves you more than you can imagine.

The God who dwells in heaven is willing to dwell also in the heart of the humble believer.

Warren Wiersbe

Honesty Begins at Home

Good people will be guided by honesty.
Proverbs 11:3 ICB

Should you be honest with your parents? Certainly. With your brothers and sisters? Of course. With cousins, grandparents, aunts and uncles? Yes! In fact, you should be honest with everybody in your family because honesty starts at home.

If you can't be honest in your own house, how can you expect to be honest in other places, like at church or at school? So make sure that you're completely honest with your family. If you are, then you're much more likely to be honest with everybody else.

Kid's Tip: It's better to say nothing: If you're tempted to say something that isn't true, don't say anything. A closed mouth tells no lies.

When Bad Things Happen

I leave you peace; my peace I give you.
I do not give it to you as the world does.
So don't let your hearts be troubled or afraid.

John 14:27 NCV

When bad things happen, it's understandable that we might feel afraid. In fact, it's good to be afraid if our fears keep us from behaving foolishly (by the way, if that little voice inside your head tells you that doing something is dangerous, don't do it).

When our own troubles—or the world's troubles—leave us fearful, we should discuss our concerns with the people who love and care for us. Parents and grandparents can help us understand our fears, and they can help us feel better. That's why we need to talk with them.

It's okay to be afraid—all of us are fearful from time to time. And it's good to know that we can talk about our fears with loved ones and with God. When we do, we'll discover that fear lasts for a little while, but love lasts forever.

Follow Jesus

Follow Me, Jesus told them,
"and I will make you into fishers of men!"
Immediately they left their nets and followed Him.
Mark 1:17-18 Holman CSB

Who will you walk with today? Do yourself a favor—walk with Jesus!

God's Word promises that when you follow in Christ's footsteps, you will learn how to behave yourself, and you'll learn how to live a good life. Jesus wants you to be a "new creation" through Him. And that's exactly what you should want for yourself, too. So talk with Jesus (through prayer) and walk with Him (by obeying His rules) today and forever.

Kid's Tip: If You Want to be a Disciple of Christ . . . follow in His footsteps, obey His commandments, talk with Him often, tell others about Him, and share His never-ending love.

Today's Ideas About
Respecting Your Parents

Here are two important ideas. Take a few minutes
to talk to your mom or dad about what these
quotations mean.

Never underestimate the power
that comes when a parent pleads
with God on behalf of a child.

Max Lucado

The children taught me much as they
were growing up: about themselves,
about the world around them, about me,
and especially about God.

Ruth Bell Graham

A GREAT BIG THANK YOU

Praise the LORD. Give thanks to the LORD,
for he is good; his love endures forever.

Psalm 106:1 NIV

If you're like most kids, you're very busy doing things and learning things. But no matter how busy you are—even if you hardly have a moment to spare—you should still slow down and say "Thank You," to God!

God has given you many things, and you owe Him everything, including a GREAT BIG THANK YOU, starting now (and ending never!)

Kid's Tip: In good times or difficult times, it is important to understand the need to praise God.

Try to Memorize This Verse

He has showed you, O man, what is good.
And what does the LORD require of you?
To act justly and to love mercy
and to walk humbly with your God.

Micah 6:8 NIV

This is an important Bible verse.
Practice saying it several times. And then, talk to
mom or dad about exactly what the verse means . . .

A Tip for Parents: Talk to your child about . . .

How God wants you to live

Think About What's Right

Keep your eyes focused on what is right.
Keep looking straight ahead to what is good.
Proverbs 4:25 ICB

In the Book of Proverbs, King Solomon gave us wonderful advice for living wisely. Solomon said that we should keep our eyes "focused on what is right." In other words, we should do our best to say and do the things that we know are pleasing to God.

The next time you're tempted to say an unkind word or to say something that isn't true, remember the advice of King Solomon. Solomon knew that it's always better to do the right thing, even when it's tempting to do otherwise. So if you know something is wrong, don't do it; instead, do what you know to be right. When you do, you'll be saving yourself a lot of trouble and you'll be obeying the Word of God.

Kid's Tip: Study God's Word each day, and strive to understand God's teachings. Seek to live in accordance with those teachings.

The Kid in the Mirror

For you made us only a little lower than God,
and you crowned us with glory and honor.

Psalm 8:5 NLT

Do you really like the person you see when you look into the mirror? You should! After all, the person in the mirror is a very special person who is made—and loved—by God.

In fact, you are loved in many, many ways: God loves you, your parents love you, and your family loves you, for starters. So you should love yourself, too.

So here's something to think about: since God thinks you're special, and since so many people think you're special, isn't it about time for you to agree with them? Of course it is! It's time to say, "You're very wonderful and very special," to the person you see in the mirror.

Kid's Tip: God loves you . . . and you should too.

You Feel Better About Yourself When You Share

Be generous to the poor—you'll never go hungry;
shut your eyes to their needs,
and run a gauntlet of curses.

Proverbs 28:27 MSG

The more you share, the quicker you'll discover this fact: Good things happen to people (like you) who are kind enough to share the blessings that God has given them.

Sharing makes you feel better about yourself. Whether you're at home or at school, remember that the best rewards go to the kids who are kind and generous—not to the people who are unkind or stingy. So do what's right: share. You'll feel lots better about yourself when you do.

When somebody needs a helping hand, he doesn't need it tomorrow or the next day. He needs it now, and that's exactly when you should offer to help.
Good deeds, if they are really good,
happen sooner rather than later.

Marie T. Freeman

Thanking Those Who Serve

There are different kinds of gifts, but they are all from the same Spirit. There are different ways to serve but the same Lord to serve.

1 Corinthians 12:4-5 NCV

Jesus instructed His disciples to help each other. Those instructions still apply. If we are to be obedient servants of Christ, we must be willing to help those who can't help themselves. In other words, we must become "servants to all."

Some people choose careers that allow them to serve and protect our homes and our world (this includes police officers, firefighters, and those who serve in our military). These brave men and women make very big sacrifices, and we should thank them whenever we can.

So let's all offer prayers of thanks for those brave men and women who serve and protect us . . . and let's all do our best to serve other people wherever we can.

Kid's Tip: Remember the people who live under your roof: Service, like love, should begin at home and work its way out from there.

Everybody Needs to Hear Kind Words

Avoid irreverent, empty speech, for this will produce an even greater measure of godlessness.

2 Timothy 2:16 Holman CSB

Your words can help people . . . or not. Make certain that you're the kind of person who says helpful things, not hurtful things. You'll feel better about yourself when you help other people feel better about themselves.

Do you like for people to say kind words to you? Of course you do! And that's exactly how other people feel, too. That's why it's so important to say things that make people feel better, not worse.

Everybody needs to hear kind words, and that's exactly the kind of words they should hear from you!

Kid's Tip: If you don't know what to say . . . don't say anything. Sometimes, a hug works better than a whole mouthful of words.

y 142

Ideas About
Things Off
Last Minute

Here are two important ideas. Take a few minutes
to talk to your mom or dad about what these
quotations mean.

Now is the only time worth
having because, indeed,
it is the only time we have.

C. H. Spurgeon

Every time you refuse to face up
to life and its problems,
you weaken your character.

E. Stanley Jones

Think Good Thoughts

Come near to God, and God will come near to you.
You sinners, clean sin out of your lives.
You who are trying to follow God and the world
at the same time, make your thinking pure.

James 4:8 NCV

Do you try to think good thoughts about your friends, your family, and yourself? The Bible says that you should. Do you lift your hopes and your prayers to God many times each day? The Bible says that you should. Do you say "no" to people who want you to do bad things or think bad thoughts? The Bible says that you should.

The Bible teaches you to guard your thoughts against things that are hurtful or wrong. So remember this: When you turn away from bad thoughts and turn instead toward God and His Son Jesus, you will be protected . . . and you will be blessed.

Kid's Tip: Good thoughts can lead you to some very good places . . . and bad thoughts can lead elsewhere.

Try to Memorize This Verse

The fear of the Lord is a fountain of life . . . .

Proverbs 14:27 NIV

This is an important Bible verse.
Practice saying it several times. And then, talk to mom or dad about exactly what the verse means . . .

A Tip for Parents: Talk to your child about . . .

Reverence for God

Telling the Truth

Jesus answered, "I am the way
and the truth and the life. No one comes to
the Father except through me."

John 14:6 NIV

Sometimes, telling the truth is hard, but even then, it's easier to tell the truth than it is to live with the consequences of telling a lie. You see, telling a lie can be easier in the beginning, but it's always harder in the end! In the end, when people find out that you've been untruthful, they may feel hurt and you will feel embarrassed.

So make this promise to yourself, and keep it: don't let lies rob you of your happiness. Instead, tell the truth from the start. You'll be doing yourself a big favor, and you'll be obeying the Word of God.

Those who walk in truth walk in liberty.

Beth Moore

Yes, Jesus Loves You

Just as the Father has loved Me,
I also have loved you. Remain in My love.

John 15:9 Holman CSB

The Bible makes this promise: Jesus loves you. And how should that make you feel? Well, the fact that Jesus loves you should make you very happy indeed, so happy, in fact, that you try your best to do the things that Jesus wants you to do.

Jesus wants you to welcome Him into your heart, He wants you to love and obey God, and He wants you to be kind to people. These are all very good things to do . . . and the rest is up to you!

Kid's Tip: Jesus loves me, this I know . . . but how much? Here's how much: Jesus loves you so much that He gave His life so that you might live forever with Him in heaven. And how can you repay Christ's love? By accepting Him into your heart and by obeying His rules.

Choosing Wisely

I am offering you life or death, blessings or curses.
Now, choose life! . . . To choose life is to love
the Lord your God, obey him, and stay close to him.

Deuteronomy 30:19-20 NCV

Choices, choices, choices! You've got so many choices to make, and sometimes, making those choices isn't easy. At times you're torn between what you want to do and what you ought to do. When that happens, it's up to you to choose wisely . . . or else!

When you make wise choices, you are rewarded; when you make unwise choices, you must accept the consequences. It's as simple as that. So make sure that your choices are pleasing to God . . . or else!

Kid's Tip: Wise choices bring you happiness; unwise choices don't. So whenever you have a choice to make, choose wisely.

Who Controls You?

Be imitators of God, therefore,
as dearly loved children.

Ephesians 5:1 NIV

Do you try hard to control yourself? If so, that's good because God wants all His children (including you) to behave themselves.

Sometimes, it's hard to be a well-behaved person, especially if you have friends who don't behave nicely. But if your friends misbehave, don't imitate them. Instead, listen to your conscience, talk to your parents, and do the right thing . . . NOW!

Kid's Tip: Start Now: If you really want to become a well-behaved person, the best day to get started is this one.

Listen to Your Conscience

I always do my best to have a clear conscience
toward God and men.

Acts 24:16 Holman CSB

Your conscience is a little feeling that will usually
tell you what to do and when to do it. Pay
attention to that feeling, and trust it.

If you slow down and listen to your conscience,
you'll usually stay out of trouble. And if you listen to
your conscience, it won't be so hard to control your
own behavior. Why? Because most of the time, your
conscience already knows right from wrong. So don't
be in such a hurry to do things. Instead of "jumping
right in," listen to your conscience. In the end, you'll
be very glad you did.

Kid's Tip: If you're not sure what to do . . . Slow
down and listen to your conscience. That little voice
inside your head is remarkably dependable, but you
can't depend upon it if you never listen to it. So
stop, listen, and learn—your conscience is almost
always right!

See the Good in Others

See to it that no one repays evil for evil to anyone,
but always pursue what is good for
one another and for all.
1 Thessalonians 5:15 Holman CSB

Do you ever make mistakes? Of course you do!
Even if you're a very good person, you're bound
to make a mistake or two—everybody does.

When you do something you shouldn't have done,
here are some things you can do:

1. Apologize to the people you've hurt, and ask
for their forgiveness; 2. Fix the things you've
messed up or broken; 3. Don't make the same
mistake again; 4. Ask God for His forgiveness
(which, by the way, He will give to you instantly); 5.
Get busy doing something you can be proud of. 6.
Don't be too hard on yourself . . . even if you made a
mistake, you're still a very, very special person!

Kid's Tip: God forgives sin when you ask . . . so ask!
God stands ready to forgive . . . the next move is
yours.

The Gold Standard

Therefore, whatever you want others to do for you,
do also the same for them—this is the Law
and the Prophets.

Matthew 7:12 Holman CSB

The words of Matthew 7:12 remind us that, as believers in Christ, we should treat others as we wish to be treated. This is called the Golden Rule, but for Christians, it's worth much more than gold.

Do you want other people to forgive you when you make mistakes? Of course you do. And that's why you should be willing to forgive them.

The Golden Rule should be your tool for deciding how you will treat others. So use the Golden Rule as your guide for living and forgiving!

We are products of our past,
but we don't have to be prisoners of it.
God specializes in giving people a fresh start.

Rick Warren

Try to Memorize This Verse

Everything is possible to the one who believes.

Mark 9:23 Holman CSB

This is an important Bible verse.
Practice saying it several times. And then, talk to mom or dad about exactly what the verse means . . .

A Tip for Parents: Talk to your child about . . .

The importance of optimism

Be Kind

So rid yourselves of all wickedness, all deceit,
hypocrisy, envy, and all slander.
1 Peter 2:1 Holman CSB

Do you know what gossip is? It's when we say bad things about people who are not around. When we gossip, we hurt others and we hurt ourselves. That's why the Bible tells us that gossip is wrong.

Sometimes, it's tempting to say bad things about people, and when we do, it makes us feel important . . . for a while. But, after a while, the bad things that we say come back to hurt us, and of course they hurt other people, too.

So if you want to be a kind person and a good friend, don't gossip . . . and don't listen to people who do.

Kid's Tip: Watch What You Say: Don't say something behind someone's back that you wouldn't say to that person directly.

...u Think You Can

> ...ghteous man falls seven times,
> ...ut the wicked will stumble into ruin.
>
> ...roverbs 24:16 Holman CSB

If you think you can do something, then you can probably do it. If you think you can't do something, then you probably won't do it.

So remember this: if you're having a little trouble getting something done, don't get mad, don't get frustrated, don't get discouraged, and don't give up. Just keep trying . . . and believe in yourself.

When you try hard—and keep trying hard—you can really do amazing things . . . but if you quit at the first sign of trouble, you'll miss out. So here's a good rule to follow: when you have something that you want to finish, finish it . . . and finish it sooner rather than later.

Kid's Tip: The next time you find your courage tested to the limit, remember that God is as near as your next breath, and remember that He offers strength and comfort to His children.

Having Trouble Behaving Yourself? Pray About It!

Rejoice always! Pray constantly.
Give thanks in everything,
for this is God's will for you in Christ Jesus.

1 Thessalonians 5:16-18 Holman CSB

Do you really want to become a more obedient person? Then pray about it. Would you like to learn how to behave yourself a little bit better? Then pray about it. Want to be able to think about things before you get into trouble, not after? Pray for God's help.

If you have questions about whether you should do something or not, pray about it. If there is something you're worried about, ask God to comfort you. And as you pray more, you'll discover that God is always near and that He's always ready to hear from you. So don't worry about things; pray about them. God is waiting to hear from you . . . so what are you waiting for?

Kid's Tip: Pray any time you can.

What Is Patience?

Therefore, God's chosen ones, holy and loved,
put on heartfelt compassion, kindness, humility,
gentleness, and patience.

Colossians 3:12 Holman CSB

The dictionary defines the word *patience* as "the ability to be calm, tolerant, and understanding." Here's what that means: the word "calm" means being in control of your emotions (not letting your emotions control you). The word "tolerant" means being kind and considerate to people who are different from you. And, the word "understanding" means being able to put yourself in another person's shoes.

If you can be calm, tolerant, and understanding, you will be the kind of person whose good deeds are a blessing to your family and friends. And that's exactly the kind of person that God wants you to be.

Kid's Tip: The best things in life seldom happen overnight . . . they usually take time.

The Right Thing

For the Kingdom of God is not just fancy talk;
it is living by God's power.
1 Corinthians 4:20 NLT

Doing the right thing is not always easy, especially when we're tired or frustrated. But, doing the wrong thing almost always leads to trouble. And sometimes, it leads to BIG trouble.

When you do the right thing, you don't have to worry about what you did or what you said. But, if you are dishonest—or if you do something that you know is wrong—you'll be worried that someone will find out. So do the right thing; it may be harder in the beginning, but it's easier in the end.

Kid's Tip: When you choose to do the right thing . . . you make everybody happy. You make your parents happy; you make your teachers happy; you make your friends happy; and you make God happy!

Today's Ideas About
Being Joyful

Here are two important ideas. Take a few minutes to talk to your mom or dad about what these quotations mean.

The joy of the Holy Spirit is experienced by giving thanks in all situations.

Bill Bright

Our sense of joy, satisfaction, and fulfillment in life increases, no matter what the circumstances, if we are in the center of God's will.

Billy Graham

The Time to Talk to God Is Now

Then if my people who are called by my name will
humble themselves and pray and seek my face
and turn from their wicked ways, I will hear from
heaven and will forgive their sins and heal their land.

2 Chronicles 7:14 NLT

God promises that He hears your prayers—every one of them! So if you want to say something to God, you can start praying (with your eyes open or shut).

Whatever your need, no matter how great or small, pray about it and never lose hope. God is not just near; He is here, and He's ready to talk with you. Now!

Kid's Tip: Sometimes, the answer to prayer is "No." God doesn't grant all of our requests, nor should He.

Don't Be Afraid to Ask Questions

When doubts filled my mind,
your comfort gave me renewed hope and cheer.

Psalm 94:19 NLT

When you're not sure about something, are you willing to ask your parents what you should do? Hopefully, when you have a question, you're not afraid to ask.

If you've got lots of questions, the Bible promises that God—like your parents—has answers, too.

So don't ever be afraid to ask questions. Both your parents and your Heavenly Father want to hear your questions . . . and they want to answer your questions as soon as you ask.

Kid's Tip: When in doubt, ask mom or dad: If you're not sure whether or not something is right or wrong, ask your parents before you do it!

Self-Control Matters

So prepare your minds for service and have
self-control. All your hope should be for
the gift of grace that will be yours when
Jesus Christ is shown to you.

1 Peter 1:13 NCV

Learning how to control yourself is an important part of growing up. The more you learn about self-control, the better. Self-control will help you at home, at school, and at church. That's why parents and teachers are happy to talk about the rewards of good self-control. And that's why you should be excited about learning how important it is to look before you leap . . . not after!

Kid's Tip: Controlling yourself by slowing yourself down: Sometimes, the best way to control yourself is to slow yourself down. Then, you can think about the things you're about to do before you do them.

Today's Ideas About
Self-Control

Here are two important ideas. Take a few minutes to talk to your mom or dad about what these quotations mean.

Your thoughts are the determining factor
as to whose mold you are conformed to.
Control your thoughts and you
control the direction of your life.

Charles Stanley

God nowhere tells us to give up things for
the sake of giving them up. He tells us to give
them up for the sake of the only thing
worth having—life with Himself.

Oswald Chambers

Think Before You Speak

To everything there is a season . . .
a time to keep silence, and a time to speak.
Ecclesiastes 3:1,7 KJV

Sometimes, it's easier to say the wrong thing than it is to say the right thing—especially if we're in a hurry to blurt out the first words that come into our heads. But, if we are patient and if we choose our words carefully, we can help other people feel better, and that's exactly what God wants us to do.

The Book of Proverbs tells us that the right words, spoken at the right time, can be wonderful gifts to our families and to our friends. That's why we should think about the things that we say before we say them, not after. When we do, our words make the world a better place, and that's exactly what God wants!

Kid's Tip: Like Momma used to say, "If you can't think of something nice to say . . . don't say anything." Sometimes, the best use of a mouth is to keep it closed.

Today's Ideas About
What to Do
When Friends Misbehave

Here are two important ideas. Take a few minutes
to talk to your mom or dad about what these
quotations mean.

God has a plan for your friendships
because He knows your friends
determine the quality
and direction of your life.

Charles Stanley

A friend is one who makes me
do my best.

Oswald Chambers

Time for God

I wait quietly before God, for my hope is in him.

Psalm 62:5 NLT

When it comes to spending time with God, are you a "squeezer" or a "pleaser"? Do you squeeze God into your schedule with a prayer before mealtime, or do you please God by talking to Him far more often than that? If you're wise, you'll form the habit of spending time with God every day.

Even if you're the busiest kid on Planet Earth, you can still carve out a little time for God. And when you think about it, isn't that the very least you should do?

Kid's Tip: The world is constantly vying for your attention, and sometimes the noise can be deafening. Remember the words of Elisabeth Elliot; she said, "The world is full of noise. Let us learn the art of silence, stillness, and solitude."

Jesus Can Take Care of Our Problems

Do not love the world or the things that belong
to the world. If anyone loves the world,
love for the Father is not in him.
1 John 2:15 Holman CSB

An old hymn contains the words, "This world is
not my home; I'm just passing through." Thank
goodness! This crazy world can be a place of trouble
and danger. Thankfully, your real home is heaven, a
place where you can live forever with Jesus.

In John 16:33, Jesus tells us He has overcome
the troubles of this world. We should trust Him,
and we should obey His commandments. When we do,
we are forever blessed by the Son of God and His
Father in heaven.

Kid's Tip: Whose Message? If you dwell on the
world's message you're setting yourself up for
disaster. If you dwell on God's message, then you're
setting yourself up for victory.

Giving Thanks

Our prayers for you are always spilling over into thanksgivings. We can't quit thanking God our Father and Jesus our Messiah for you!

Colossians 1:3 MSG

Are you a thankful person? You should be! Whether you realize it or not, you have much to be thankful for. And who has given you all the blessings you enjoy? Your parents are responsible, of course. But all of our blessings really start with God.

All of us should make thanksgiving a habit. Since we have been given so much, the least we can do is say "Thank You" to the One who has given us more blessings than we can possibly ever count.

Kid's Tip: When is the best time to say "thanks" to God? Any Time. God loves you all the time, and that's exactly why you should praise Him all the time.

If You're Trying to Be Perfect

The Lord says, "Forget what happened before, and do not think about the past. Look at the new thing I am going to do. It is already happening. Don't you see it? I will make a road in the desert and rivers in the dry land."

Isaiah 43:18-19 NCV

If you're trying to be perfect, you're trying to do something that's impossible. No matter how much you try, you can't be a perfect person . . . and that's okay.

God doesn't expect you to live a mistake-free life—and neither should you. In the game of life, God expects you to try, but He doesn't always expect you to win. Sometimes, you'll make mistakes, but even then, you shouldn't give up!

So remember this: you don't have to be perfect to be a wonderful person. In fact, you don't even need to be "almost-perfect". You simply must try your best and leave the rest up to God.

Kid's Tip: Don't be too hard on yourself: you don't have to be perfect to be wonderful.

Slowing Down for God!

Don't burn out; keep yourselves fueled and aflame.
Be alert servants of the Master,
cheerfully expectant. Don't quit in hard times;
pray all the harder.

Romans 12:11-12 MSG

Everybody knows you're a very busy kid. But here's a question: are you able to squeeze time into your schedule for God? Hopefully so!

Nothing is more important than the time you spend with your Heavenly Father. So take some time today and every day to pray and to thank God for His blessings. God will be glad you did, and you'll be glad, too.

How busy we have become . . .
and as a result, how empty!

Charles Swindoll

God's House

For where two or three are gathered together
in My name, I am there among them.

Matthew 18:20 Holman CSB

When your parents take you to church, are you pleased to go? Hopefully so. After all, church is a wonderful place to learn about God's rules.

The church belongs to God just as surely as you belong to God. That's why the church is a good place to learn about God and about His Son Jesus.

So when your mom and dad take you to church, remember this: church is a fine place to be . . . and you're lucky to be there.

Kid's Tip: Forget the Excuses: If somebody starts making up reasons not to go to church, don't pay any attention . . . even if that person is you!

Moving On

Mockers can get a whole town agitated,
but those who are wise will calm anger.
Proverbs 29:8 NLT

Today and every day, make sure that you're a person who is known for the kind way that you treat everybody. That's how God wants you to behave.

And if someone says something to you that isn't very nice, don't pay too much attention. Just forgive that person as quickly as you can, and try to move on . . . as quickly as you can.

We are all fallen creatures
and all very hard to live with.
C. S. Lewis

Keep the Peace

Love must be without hypocrisy. Detest evil;
cling to what is good. Show family affection to
one another with brotherly love.
Outdo one another in showing honor.

Romans 12:9-10 Holman CSB

Sometimes, it's easiest to become angry with the
people we love the most. After all, we know that
they'll still love us no matter how angry we become.
But while it's easy to become angry at home, it's
usually wrong.

The next time you're tempted to become angry
with a brother, or a sister, or a parent, remember
that these are the people who love you more than
anybody else! Then, calm down. Because peace is
always beautiful, especially when it's peace at your
house.

Kid's Tip: What if you're having really big problems
with your family? You've simply got to keep talking
things over, even if it's hard. And, remember: what
seems like a mountain today may turn out to be a
molehill tomorrow.

Forgiveness Can Be Hard

Anyone who claims to live in God's light
and hates a brother or sister is still in the dark.

1 John 2:9 MSG

Sometimes, it's very hard! But God tells us that we must forgive other people, even when we'd rather not. So, if you're angry with anybody (or if you're upset by something you yourself have done) it's time to forgive. Right now!

But what if you have already tried to forgive somebody yet simply can't do it? Then you must keep trying. If you can't seem to forgive someone, you should keep asking God to help you until you do. And you can be sure of this: if you keep asking for God's help, He will give it.

Kid's Tip: Because God has forgiven you, you can forgive yourself.

Day 174

Kind Thoughts

Whoever forgives someone's sin makes a friend,
but gossiping about the sin breaks up friendships.

Proverbs 17:9 NCV

What does it mean to forgive? Forgiveness means that you decide to change your angry thoughts into kind thoughts. Forgiveness means that you decide not to stay mad at somebody who has done something wrong. Forgiveness happens when you decide that obeying God is more important than staying angry.

Sometimes forgiveness can be very hard, but it's the right thing to do. Why? Because forgiveness is God's way, and you should make it your way, too!

We cannot be right with God
until we are right with one another.

Charles Swindoll

Today's Ideas About Jesus

Here are two important ideas. Take a few minutes to talk to your mom or dad about what these quotations mean.

When we are in a situation where Jesus is all we have, we soon discover He is all we really need.

Gigi Graham Tchividjian

There is not a single thing that Jesus cannot change, control, and conquer because He is the living Lord.

Franklin Graham

Perfect Love

For God so loved the world that he gave
his only Son, so that everyone who believes in him
will not perish but have eternal life.

John 3:16 NLT

The Bible makes this promise: God is love. It's a big promise, a very important description of what God is and how God works. God's love is perfect. When we open our hearts to His love, we are blessed and we are protected.

Today, offer sincere prayers of thanksgiving to your Heavenly Father. He loves you now and throughout all eternity. Open your heart to His presence and His love.

Kid's Tip: God's love makes everything look a lot better: When you invite the love of God into your heart, everything in the world looks different, including you.

Trusting God

> "I say this because I know what I am planning for you," says the Lord. "I have good plans for you, not plans to hurt you. I will give you hope and a good future."
>
> Jeremiah 29:11 NCV

Sometimes, things happen that we simply don't understand. And that's exactly how God intends it! You see God has given us many gifts, but He hasn't given us the power to understand everything that happens in our world (that comes later, when we get to heaven!)

The Bible tells us God's plans are far bigger than we humans can possibly understand. That's one of the reasons that God doesn't make His plans clear to us. But even when we can't understand why God allows certain things to happen, we can trust His love for us.

The Bible does make one part of God's plan perfectly clear: we should accept His Son Jesus into our hearts so that we might have eternal life (John 3:16). And when we do, we are protected today, tomorrow, and forever.

Honesty Pays

If you really carry out the royal law prescribed in
Scripture, You shall love your neighbor
as yourself, you are doing well.

James 2:8 Holman CSB

Do you want other people to be honest with you?
Of course you do. And that's why you should
be honest with them. The words of Matthew 7:12
remind us that, as believers in Christ, we should
treat others as we wish to be treated. And that
means telling them the truth!

The Golden Rule is your tool for deciding how you
will treat other people. When you use the Golden
Rule as your guide for living, your words and your
actions will be pleasing to other people and to God.

Kid's Tip: It is important to treat all people with
respect and kindness.

Try to Memorize This Verse

But the fruit of the Spirit is love, joy, peace, patience, kindness, goodness, faith, gentleness, self-control. Against such things there is no law.

Galatians 5:22-23 Holman CSB

This is an important Bible verse.
Practice saying it several times. And then, talk to mom or dad about exactly what the verse means . . .

A Tip for Parents: Talk to your child about . . .

Fruit of the Spirit

...vays the Right Thing to Do

> Tell each other the truth because we all
> belong to each other . . . .
> Ephesians 4:25 ICB

It's important to be honest. When you tell the truth, you'll feel better about yourself, and other people will feel better about you, too. But that's not all. When you tell the truth, God knows—and He will reward you for your honesty.

Telling the truth is hard sometimes. But it's better to be honest, even when it's hard. So remember this: telling the truth is always the right thing to do . . . always.

Kid's Tip: White lies? Beware! Sometimes, we're tempted to "shade" the truth. Unfortunately, little white lies have a tendency to turn black . . . and they grow. The best strategy is to avoid untruths of all sizes and colors.

Today's Ideas About
Asking God

Here are two important ideas. Take a few minutes to talk to your mom or dad about what these quotations mean.

God uses our most stumbling, faltering faith-steps as the open door to His doing for us "more than we ask or think."

Catherine Marshall

Some people think God does not like to be troubled with our constant asking. But, the way to trouble God is not to come at all.

D. L. Moody

God cares about everything in your life — even the little things.

It's Not Hard to Be Kind

Therefore, God's chosen ones, holy and loved,
put on heartfelt compassion, kindness, humility,
gentleness, and patience.

Colossians 3:12 Holman CSB

How hard is it to say a kind word? Not very! Yet sometimes we're so busy that we forget to say the very things that might make other people feel better.

We should always try to say nice things to our families and friends. And when we feel like saying something that's not so nice, perhaps we should stop and think before we say it. Kind words help; cruel words hurt. It's as simple as that. And, when we say the right thing at the right time, we give a gift that can change someone's day or someone's life.

Kid's Tip: It's good to tell your family how you feel about them, but that's not enough. You should also show them how you feel with your good deeds and your kind words.

Listen to Your Parents

Listen carefully to wisdom;
set your mind on understanding.
Proverbs 2:2 NCV

Do you listen carefully to the things your parents tell you? You should. Your parents want the very best for you. They want you to be happy and healthy; they want you to be smart and to do smart things. Your parents have much to teach you, and you have much to learn. So listen carefully to the things your mom and dad have to say. And ask lots of questions. When you do, you'll soon discover that your parents have lots of answers . . . lots of very good answers.

Listening is loving.
Zig Ziglar

God Teaches Us

If you hide your sins, you will not succeed.
If you confess and reject them,
you will receive mercy.
Proverbs 28:13 NCV

The Bible says that when people make mistakes, God corrects them. And that means that if you make a mistake, God will try to find a way to teach you how to keep from making that same mistake again.

God doesn't expect you to be perfect, but He does expect you to learn from your mistakes—NOW!

Kid's Tip: When you make a mistake, learn something . . . and forgive someone: yourself. Remember, you don't have to be perfect to be wonderful.

The Best Time to Be Obedient

The one who has My commandments and keeps them
is the one who loves Me. And the one who
loves Me will be loved by My Father.
I also will love him and will reveal Myself to him.
John 14:21 Holman CSB

If you look in a dictionary, you'll see that the word "wisdom" means "using good judgement, and knowing what is true," But there's more: it's not enough just to know what's right; if you really want to become a wise person, you must also do what's right.

A big part of "doing what's right" is learning to be obedient . . . and the best time to start being a more obedient person is right now! Why? Because it's the wise thing to do.

Kid's Tip: Do not willingly put yourself in situations where you might be easily tempted to disobey God.

ence and the Golden Rule

Always be humble and gentle.
Be patient and accept each other with love.

Ephesians 4:2 ICB

Jesus gave us a Golden Rule for living: He said that we should treat other people in the same way that we want to be treated. And because we want other people to be patient with us, we, in turn, must be patient with them.

Being patient with other people means treating them with kindness, respect, and understanding. It means waiting our turn when we're standing in line and forgiving our friends when they've done something we don't like. Sometimes, it's hard to be patient, but we've got to do our best. And when we do, we're following the Golden Rule—God's rule for how to treat others—and everybody wins!

Kid's Tip: Patience is not idly waiting but it is an activity that means watching and waiting for God to lead you.

When Friends Misbehave

Whoever walks with the wise will become wise;
whoever walks with fools will suffer harm.

Proverbs 13:20 NLT

If you're like most people, you have probably been tempted to "go along with the crowd" . . . even when the crowd was misbehaving. But here's something to think about: just because your friends may be misbehaving doesn't mean that you have to misbehave, too.

When people behave badly, they can spoil things in a hurry. So make sure that they don't spoil things for you.

So, if your friends misbehave, don't copy them! Instead, do the right thing. You'll be glad you did . . . and so will God!

Kid's Tip: Remember that it's more important to be respected than to be liked.

You Can't Please Everybody

My son, if sinners entice you, don't be persuaded.
Proverbs 1:10 Holman CSB

Are you one of those people who tries to please everybody in sight? If so, you'd better watch out! After all, if you worry too much about pleasing your friends, you may not worry enough about pleasing God.

Whom will you try to please today: your God or your pals? The answer to that question should be simple. Your first job is to obey God's rules . . . and that means obeying your parents, too!

So don't worry too much about pleasing your friends or neighbors. Try, instead, to please your heavenly Father and your parents. No exceptions.

Kid's Tip: You simply cannot please everybody. So here's what you should do: Try pleasing God and your parents.

Practicing Forgiveness

Smart people know how to hold their tongue;
their grandeur is to forgive and forget.

Proverbs 19:11 MSG

Forgiving other people requires practice and lots
of it. So when it comes to forgiveness, here's
something you should remember: if at first you don't
succeed, don't give up!

Are you having trouble forgiving someone
(or, for that matter, forgiving yourself for a
mistake that you've made)? If so, remember that
forgiveness isn't easy, so keep trying until you get it
right . . . and if you keep trying, you can be sure that
sooner or later, you will get it right.

Kid's Tip: For most of us—kids and grown-ups
alike—forgiveness doesn't come naturally. Keep
practicing until it does.

Try to Memorize This Verse

For where two or three
are gathered together in My name,
I am there among them.

Matthew 18:20 Holman CSB

This is an important Bible verse.
Practice saying it several times. And then, talk to
mom or dad about exactly what the verse means . . .

A Tip for Parents: Talk to your child about . . .

The presence of God

Be the Right Kind of Christian

The one who plants and the one who waters have
the same purpose, and each will be rewarded
for his own work.

1 Corinthians 3:8 NCV

Do you want to be the kind of Christian that God
intends for you to be? It's up to you! You'll be
the one who will decide how you behave.

If you decide to obey God and trust His Son,
you will be rewarded now and forever. So guard your
heart and trust your heavenly Father. He will never
lead you astray.

Kid's Tip: It's easy to blame others when you get
into trouble . . . but it's wrong. Instead of trying to
blame other people for your own misbehavior, take
responsibility . . . and learn from your mistakes!

ove Yourself, Too!

Goa began doing a good work in you,
and I am sure he will continue it until it is finished
when Jesus Christ comes again.

Philippians 1:6 NCV

The Bible teaches you this lesson: you should love everybody—and the word "everybody" includes yourself. Do you treat yourself with honor and respect? You should. After all, God created you in a very special way, and He loves you very much. And if God thinks you are amazing and wonderful, shouldn't you think about yourself in the same way? Of course you should!

So remember this: God wants you to love everybody, including the person you see when you look in the mirror. And one more thing: when you learn how to respect the person in the mirror, you'll be better at respecting other people, too.

Kid's Tip: When you learn about the Bible, you'll learn how much God loves you.

Learning How to Share

He that giveth, let him do it with simplicity . . . .
Romans 12:8 KJV

If you're having a little trouble learning how to share your stuff, you're not alone! Most people have problems letting go of things, so don't be discouraged. Just remember that learning to share requires practice and lots of it. The more you share—and the more you learn how good it feels to share—the sooner you'll be able to please God with the generosity and love that flows from your heart.

The mind grows by taking in,
but the heart grows by giving out.
Warren Wiersbe

Today's Ideas About
Respecting Other People

Here are two important ideas. Take a few minutes
to talk to your mom or dad about what these
quotations mean.

If you are willing to honor a person
out of respect for God, you can be
assured that God will honor you.

Beth Moore

Don't be a half-Christian.
There are too many of them in
the world already. The world has
a profound respect for a person
who is sincere in his faith.

Billy Graham

Sharing Is Better Than Being Stingy

And God will generously provide all you need.
Then you will always have everything you need and
plenty left over to share with others.

2 Corinthians 9:8 NLT

The Bible teaches that it's better to be generous than selfish. But sometimes, you won't feel like sharing your things, and you'll be tempted to keep everything for yourself. When you're feeling a little bit stingy, remember this: God wants you to share your things, and He will reward you when you do so.

When you learn to be a more generous person, God will be pleased with you . . . and you'll be pleased with yourself. So do yourself (and everybody else) a favor: be a little more generous, starting NOW!

Kid's Tip: When you are generous with others, God blesses you even more.

Day 196

Be careful what you see, hear, & speak

Today's Ideas About
The Things You See on TV

Here are two important ideas. Take a few minutes
to talk to your mom or dad about what these
quotations mean.

It is impossible to please God
doing things motivated by
and produced by the flesh.
Bill Bright

Bad influences in the world

The world's sewage system threatens
to contaminate the stream of
Christian thought. Is the world shaping
your mind, or is Christ?
Billy Graham

Putting God First

Do not have other gods besides Me.

Exodus 20:3 Holman CSB

Are you willing to put God first, or do you put other things ahead of your love for Him? God wants you to love Him first, and He wants you to obey Him first. When you do these things, you'll be happy you did!

When the Pharisees quizzed Jesus about God's most important commandment, Jesus answered, "Love the Lord your God with all your heart, all your soul, and all your mind. This is the first and most important command" (Matthew 22:37-38 NCV). So if you want to do the right thing, always put Him in the place He deserves: first place.

Kid's Tip: Talk to your parents about ways you can put God in first place.

Peace at Home

My dear brothers, always be willing to listen and
slow to speak. Do not become angry easily.
Anger will not help you live a good life as God wants.

James 1:19 ICB

Sometimes, it's easy to become angry with the
people we love most, and sometimes it's hard
to forgive them. After all, we know that our family
will still love us no matter how angry we become. But
while it's easy to become angry at home, it's usually
wrong.

The next time you're tempted to stay angry
at a brother, or a sister, or a parent, remember
that these are the people who love you more than
anybody else! Then, calm down, and forgive them . . .
NOW! Because peace is always beautiful, especially
when it's peace at your house.

When you strike out in anger, you may miss
the other person, but you will always hit yourself.

Jim Gallery

The Blame Game

People's own foolishness ruins their lives,
but in their minds they blame the Lord.

Proverbs 19:3 NCV

When something goes wrong, do you look for somebody to blame? And do you try to blame other people even if you're the one who made the mistake? Hopefully not!

It's silly to try to blame other people for your own mistakes, so don't do it.

If you've done something you're ashamed of, don't look for somebody to blame; look for a way to say, "I'm sorry, and I won't make that same mistake again."

Kid's Tip: Don't play the blame game: it's very tempting to blame others when you make a mistake, but it's more honest to look in the mirror first.

What Your Conscience Says About Forgiveness

Now the goal of our instruction is love from
a pure heart, a good conscience, and a sincere faith.

1 Timothy 1:5 Holman CSB

God gave you something called a conscience:
it's that little feeling that tells you whether
something is right or wrong. Your conscience will
usually tell you what to do and when to do it. Trust
that feeling.

If you listen to your conscience, it won't be
as hard for you to forgive people. Why? Because
forgiving other people is the right thing to do. And,
it's what God want's you to do. And it's what your
conscience tells you to do. So what are you waiting
for?

Kid's Tip: Trust the quiet inner voice of your
conscience: Treat your conscience as you would a
trusted advisor. (Luke 17:21)

When People Are Cruel

A kind man benefits himself,
but a cruel man brings disaster on himself.

Proverbs 11:17 Holman CSB

Face it: sometimes people can be cruel. And when people are unkind to you or to your friends, you may be tempted to strike back in anger. Don't do it! Instead, remember that God corrects other people's behaviors in His own way, and He doesn't need your help. So even when other people misbehave, God wants you to forgive them . . . and that's what you should do.

Kid's Tip: Stand up and be counted! Do you know children who say or do cruel things to other kids? If so, don't join in! Instead, stand up for those who need your help. It's the right thing to do.

Loving People Who Are Hard to Love

You have heard it said, "Love your neighbor and hate your enemy." But I tell you: Love your enemies and pray for those who persecute you, that you may be sons of your Father in heaven.

Matthew 5:43-45 NIV

Sometimes people can be rude . . . very rude. As long as you live here on earth, you will face countless opportunities to lose your temper when other folks behave badly. But God has a better plan: He wants you to forgive people and move on. Remember that God has already forgiven you, so it's only right that you should be willing to forgive others.

So here's some good advice: Forgive everybody as quickly as you can, and leave the rest up to God.

You can be sure you are abiding in Christ if you are able to have a Christlike love toward the people that irritate you the most.

Vonette Bright

How Do They Know?

Do you want to be counted wise, to build
a reputation for wisdom? Here's what you do:
Live well, live wisely, live humbly. It's the way you
live, not the way you talk, that counts.

James 3:13 MSG

How do people know that you're a Christian?
Well, you can tell them, of course. And make
no mistake about it: talking about your faith in God
is a very good thing to do. But simply telling people
about Jesus isn't enough. You must also be willing to
show people how a real Christian (like you) should
behave. Does that sound like a big responsibility? It
is . . . but you can do it!

Kid's Tip: The life you live is your most important
testimony.

Willing to Forgive

Talk and act like a person expecting to be judged by the Rule that sets us free. For if you refuse to act kindly, you can hardly expect to be treated kindly. Kind mercy wins over harsh judgment every time.

James 2:12-13 MSG

The Bible tells us this: When other people do things that are wrong, we should forgive them. God's Word also tells us that when we're willing to forgive others, God is quick to forgive us for the mistakes that we make.

Has somebody done something that makes you angry? Talk things over with your mom or dad, and then be ready to forgive the person who has hurt your feelings. And remember: God wants you to hurry up and forgive others, just like God is always in a hurry to forgive you.

Kid's Tip: If forgiveness were easy, everybody would be doing it—but it's not always easy to forgive and forget. If you simply can't seem to forgive somebody, pray about it . . . and keep praying about it . . . until God helps you do the right thing.

Positive Peer Pressure

My dear, dear friends, if God loved us like this,
we certainly ought to love each other.

1 John 4:11 MSG

Are your friends the kind of kids who encourage you to behave yourself? If so, you've chosen your friends wisely.

But if your friends try to get you in trouble, perhaps it's time to think long and hard about making some new friends.

Whether you know it or not, you're probably going to behave like your friends behave. So pick out friends who make you want to behave better, not worse. When you do, you'll be saving yourself from a lot of trouble . . . a whole lot of trouble.

Kid's Tip: Choose wise friends, and listen carefully to the advice that they give.

Try to Memorize This Verse

A gentle answer turns away wrath,
but a harsh word stirs up anger.
Proverbs 15:1 NIV

This is an important Bible verse.
Practice saying it several times. And then, talk to
mom or dad about exactly what the verse means . . .

A Tip for Parents: Talk to your child about . . .

The words they speak

Your Picture

For God so loved the world that he gave his
only Son, so that everyone who believes in him
will not perish but have eternal life.

John 3:16 NLT

If God had a refrigerator in heaven, your picture
would be on it! And that fact should make you
feel very good about the person you are and the
person you can become.

God's love for you is bigger and more wonderful
than you can imagine. So do this, and do it right
now: accept God's love with open arms and welcome
His Son Jesus into your heart. When you do, you'll
feel better about yourself . . . and your life will be
changed forever.

Kid's Tip: Remember: God's love for you is too big to
understand with your brain . . . but it's not too big to
feel with your heart.

Day 208

He Is Everywhere

God did this so that men would seek him
and perhaps reach out for him and find him,
though he is not far from each one of us.

Acts 17:27 NIV

God is everywhere you have ever been. And He is everywhere you will ever go. That's why you can speak to God any time you need to.

If you are afraid or discouraged, you can turn to God for strength. If you are worried, you can trust God's promises. And if you are happy, you can thank Him for His gifts.

God is right here, and so are you. And He's waiting patiently to hear from you, so why not have a word with Him right now?

Kid's Tip: Seek God's presence and wisdom allowing Him to influence your decisions throughout the day.

The Good in Others, and You

Dear friend, do not imitate what is evil,
but what is good. The one who does good is of God;
the one who does evil has not seen God.

3 John 1:11 Holman CSB

If you look for the good in other people, you'll probably find it. And, if you look for the good things in life, you'll probably find them, too.

But if you spend your time looking for things that aren't so good, you'll most certainly find plenty of bad things to look at. So what should you do? It's simple: you should look for the good things. When you do, you'll find them everywhere: in church, at school, in your neighborhood, and at home.

So don't waste your time on things that make you feel angry, discouraged, worried, guilty, or afraid. Look, instead, for the good things in life, the things that God wants you to pay attention to. You'll be glad you did . . . and God will be glad, too.

Do all the good you can. By all the means you can.
In all the ways you can. In all the places you can.
At all the times you can. To all the people you can.
As long as ever you can.

John Wesley

Each Day Is a Gift

How happy are those who can live in your house,
always singing your praises. How happy are those
who are strong in the Lord . . . .

Psalm 84:4-5 NLT

God wants you to have a happy, joyful life. But
that doesn't mean that you'll be happy all the
time. Sometimes, you won't feel like feeling happy,
and when you don't, your attitude won't be very
good.

When you're feeling a little tired or sad, here's
something to remember: This day is a gift from God.
And it's up to you to enjoy this day by trying to be
cheerful, helpful, courteous, and well behaved. How
can you do these things? A good place to start is by
doing your best to think good thoughts.

Kid's Tip: To make happiness last, we must obey God
while celebrating His blessings. To make happiness
disappear, we need only disobey God while ignoring
His blessings.

A Royal Law

This royal law is found in the Scriptures:
"Love your neighbor as yourself."
If you obey this law, then you are doing right.

James 2:8 ICB

James was the brother of Jesus and a leader of the early Christian church. In a letter that is now a part of the New Testament, James reminded his friends of a "royal law." That law is the Golden Rule.

When we treat others in the same way that we wish to be treated, we are doing the right thing. James knew it and so, of course did his brother Jesus. Now we should learn the same lesson: it's nice to be nice; it's good to be good; and it's great to be kind.

Encouraging others means helping people, looking for the best in them, and trying to bring out their positive qualities.

John Maxwell

His Joy, Our Joy

I've told you these things for a purpose:
that my joy might be your joy,
and your joy wholly mature.

John 15:11 MSG

Christ made it clear to His followers: He intended that His joy would become their joy. And it still holds true today: Christ intends that His believers share His love with His joy in their hearts. Yet sometimes, amid the inevitable hustle and bustle of life-here-on-earth, we can forfeit—albeit temporarily—the joy of Christ as we wrestle with the challenges of daily living.

C. H. Spurgeon, the 19th-century English clergymen, advised, "The Lord is glad to open the gate to every knocking soul. It opens very freely. Have faith and enter at this moment through holy courage. If you knock with a heavy heart, you shall yet sing with joy of spirit. Never be discouraged!" How true!

Kid's Tip: Joy does not depend upon circumstances, but on your relationship with God.

Listen Up!

A wise man will hear and increase in learning,
and a man of understanding will acquire wise counsel.
Proverbs 1:5 NASB

Have you learned how to sit quietly and listen to your parents and your teachers? Have you learned how to listen respectfully—with your ears open wide and your mouth closed tight? If so, give yourself a big pat on the back (or if you can't reach way back there, ask your mom or dad to do it for you!)

An important part of learning self-control is learning how to be quiet when you're supposed to be quiet. It isn't always easy, but the sooner you learn how to sit quietly and behave respectfully, the better. So you might as well start today.

Kid's Tip: Listen first, then speak: For most people, the temptation to talk is great; it takes conscious effort to hold one's tongue until one's ears are fully engaged. When a person is able to do so, his or her efforts are usually rewarded.

How Much Is Too Much?

Since we entered the world penniless and will leave it penniless, if we have bread on the table and shoes on our feet, that's enough.

1 Timothy 6:7-8 MSG

How much stuff is too much stuff? Well, if your desire for stuff is getting in the way of your desire to know God, then you've got too much stuff—it's as simple as that.

If you find yourself worrying too much about stuff, it's time to change the way you think about the things you own. Stuff isn't really very important to God, and it shouldn't be too important to you.

Kid's Tip: Materialism Made Simple: The world wants you to believe that "money and stuff" can buy happiness. Don't believe it! Genuine happiness comes not from money, but from the things that money can't buy—starting, of course, with your relationship to God and His only begotten Son.

Obedience Is a Choice

Those who obey his commands live in him,
and he in them. And this is how we know that he
lives in us: We know it by the Spirit he gave us.
1 John 3:24 NIV

You have a choice to make: are you going to be an obedient person or not? And remember: the decision to be obedient—or the decision not to be obedient—is a decision that you must make for yourself.

If you decide to behave yourself you've made a smart choice. If you decide to obey your parents, you've made another smart choice. If you decide to pay attention to your teachers, you've made yet another wise choice. BUT . . . if you decide not to be obedient, you've made a silly choice.

What kind of person will you choose to be? An obedient, well-behaved person . . . or the opposite? Before you answer that question, here's something to think about: obedience pays . . . and disobedience doesn't.

Kid's Tip: When you make wise choices you make everybody happy. And, you make God happy!

Get Over It

Do not remember the past events, pay no attention
to things of old. Look, I am about to do something
new; even now it is coming. Do you not see it?
Indeed, I will make a way in the wilderness,
rivers in the desert.

Isaiah 43:18-19 Holman CSB

An important part of learning how to forgive
is learning how to get over the things that
happened yesterday. What happened yesterday is
past. And, if what happened yesterday has made
you unhappy, today is as good a day as any to start
getting over your hurt feelings.

Are you still angry with someone? Has that
person said he was sorry and tried to make things
better? If so, talk to your parents about it! They'll
help you understand that you can't change the past,
but you can get over it.

Kid's Tip: The past is past, so don't live there. If
you're focused on the past, change your focus. If
you're living in the past, it's time to stop living there.

Jesus Offers Peace

I have told you these things, so that in me you may
have peace. In this world you will have trouble.
But take heart! I have overcome the world.

John 16:33 NIV

Jesus offers us peace . . . peace in our hearts and
peace in our homes. But He doesn't force us to
enjoy His peace—we can either accept His peace or
not.

When we accept the peace of Jesus Christ by
opening up our hearts to Him, we feel much better
about ourselves, our families, and our lives.

Would you like to feel a little better about
yourself and a little better about your corner of the
world? Then open up your heart to Jesus, because
that's where real peace begins.

Kid's Tip: Peace Starts at Home . . . you have a big
role to play in helping to maintain a peaceful home.
It's a big job, so don't be afraid to ask for help . . .
especially God's help.

Nobody's Perfect

For everything created by God is good,
and nothing should be rejected if it is
received with thanksgiving.

1 Timothy 4:4 Holman CSB

Face facts: nobody's perfect . . . not even you!
And remember this: it's perfectly okay not to
be perfect. In fact, God doesn't expect you to be
perfect, and you shouldn't expect yourself to be
perfect, either.

Are you one of those people who can't stand
to make a mistake? Do you think that you must
please everybody all the time? When you make a
mess of things, do you become terribly upset? If
so, here's some advice: DON'T BE SO HARD ON
YOURSELF! Mistakes happen . . . and besides, if you
learn something from your mistakes, you'll become a
better person.

Kid's Tip: The world isn't perfect; your family and
friends aren't perfect; and you aren't perfect—and
that's okay: We'll all have plenty of time to be
perfect in heaven. Until then, we should all be
compassionate, forgiving Christians.

What's Really Important

A pretentious, showy life is an empty life;
a plain and simple life is a full life.
Proverbs 13:7 MSG

"So much stuff to shop for, and so little time . . ."
These words describe lots of people, but
please don't let those words describe you!

The Bible teaches this important lesson: it's not
good to be too concerned about money or the stuff
that money can buy. So don't worry too much about
the things you can buy in stores. Worry more about
obeying your parents and obeying your Heavenly
Father—that's what's really important.

Kid's Tip: Stuff 101: The world says, "Buy more
stuff." God says, "Stuff isn't important." Believe
God.

Try to Memorize This Verse

If we confess our sins,
He is faithful and righteous
to forgive us our sins and to cleanse us
from all unrighteousness.

1 John 1:9 Holman CSB

This is an important Bible verse.
Practice saying it several times. And then, talk to
mom or dad about exactly what the verse means . . .

A Tip for Parents: Talk to your child about . . .

The need to confess sin

Be Responsible

So then each of us shall give account
of himself to God.

Romans 14:12 NKJV

Nobody can be patient for you. You've got to be
patient for yourself. Certainly your parents
can teach you about patience, but when it comes to
controlling your temper, nobody can control it for
you; you've got to control it yourself.

In the Book of Galatians, Paul writes, "We must
not tire of doing good." And that's an important
lesson: even when we're tired or frustrated, we
must do our best to do the right thing.

So the next time you're tempted to lose your
temper, stop for a moment and remember that when
it comes to good deeds and good behavior, it's all up
to you.

Although God causes all things to work together
for good for His children, He still holds us
accountable for our behavior.

Kay Arthur

You're So Very Special

Blessed is the man who does not condemn himself.
Romans 14:22 Holman CSB

When God made you, He made you in a very special way. In fact, you're a wonderful, one-of-a-kind creation, a special person unlike any other.

Do you realize how special you are? Do you know that God loves you because of who you are (not because of the things you've done)? And do you know that God has important things for you to do? Well whether you realize it or not, all these things are all true.

So the next time you feel bad about something you've done, take a look in the mirror, and remember that you're looking at a wonderfully special person . . . you!

God loves you; your parents love you; your family loves you . . . and that's the way that you should feel about yourself, too.

Kid's Tip: God is working in you and through you to help you become the person He intends for you to be.

Do the Right Thing: Share!

Good will come to a man who lends generously
and conducts his business fairly.

Psalm 112:5 Holman CSB

It's a fact: sharing makes you a better person.
Why? Because when you share, you're doing
several things: first, you're obeying God; and, you're
making your corner of the world a better place; and
you're learning exactly what it feels like to be a
generous, loving person.

When you share, you have the fun of knowing
that your good deeds are making other people happy.
When you share, you're learning how to become a
better person. When you share, you're making things
better for other people and for yourself. So do the
right thing: share!

Find out how much God has given you
and from it take what you need;
the remainder is needed by others.

St. Augustine

Day 224

Keep Growing Up

Therefore, leaving the elementary message about
the Messiah, let us go on to maturity.

Hebrews 6:1 Holman CSB

When will you be completely grown up?
Hopefully never! God has a way of helping
you continue to grow as a Christian throughout your
entire life if you continue to worship Him.

If you learn about God's Word and talk to Him
through your prayers, He has much to teach you,
so keep learning about your Heavenly Father. And
never stop.

Kid's Tip: Regular, consistent study of God's Word
will help ensure that you will continue to grow as a
Christian . . .

Give Thanks!

And whatever you do, in word or in deed, do everything in the name of the Lord Jesus, giving thanks to God the Father through Him.

Colossians 3:17 Holman CSB

Do you have a thankful attitude? Hopefully so! After all, you've got plenty of things to be thankful for. Even during those times when you're angry or tired, you're a very lucky person.

Who has given you all the blessings you enjoy? Your parents are responsible, of course. But all of your blessings really start with God. That's why you should say "Thank You" to God many times each day. He's given you so much . . . so thank Him, starting now.

Kid's Tip: Want to cheer yourself up? Count your blessings. If you need a little cheering up, start counting your blessings . . . and keep counting until you feel better.

Waiting Your Turn

Don't be impatient for the Lord to act! Travel
steadily along his path. He will honor you . . . .
Psalm 37:34 NLT

When we're standing in line or waiting our
turn, it's tempting to scream, "Me first!"
It's tempting, but it's the wrong thing to do! The
Bible tells us that we shouldn't push ahead of other
people; instead, we should do the right thing—and
the polite thing—by saying, "You first!"

Sometimes, waiting your turn can be hard,
especially if you're excited or in a hurry. But even
then, waiting patiently is the right thing to do.
Why? Because parents say so, teachers say so, and,
most importantly, God says so!

It's not difficult to make an impact on your world.
All you really have to do is put the needs of others
ahead of your own. You can make a difference
with a little time and a big heart.

James Dobson

Truth Be Told

He has showed you, O man, what is good.
And what does the LORD require of you?
To act justly and to love mercy
and to walk humbly with your God.

Micah 6:8 NIV

If you're tempted to say something that isn't true, stop and ask yourself a simple question: "How would Jesus behave if He were here?" The answer to that question will tell you what to say.

Jesus told His followers that the truth would make them free. As believers, we must do our best to know the truth and to tell it. When we do, we behave as our Savior behaved, and that's exactly how God wants us to behave.

Kid's Tip: When in doubt: do the thing that you think Jesus would do. And, of course, don't do something if you think that He wouldn't do it.

Time with God

Careful planning puts you ahead in the long run;
hurry and scurry puts you further behind.

Proverbs 21:5 MSG

How much time do you spend getting to know God? A lot? A little? Almost none? Hopefully, you answered, "a lot."

God loved this world so much that He sent His Son to save it. And now only one real question remains for you: what will you do in response to God's love? God deserves your prayers, your obedience, and your love—and He deserves these things all day every day, not just on Sunday mornings.

Kid's Tip: You should plan to spent some time with God every day . . . and you should stick to your plan!

God Is Watching

Remember that those who do good prove that they are God's children, and those who do evil prove that they do not know God.

3 John 1:11 NLT

Even when nobody's watching, God is. And He knows whether you've done the right thing or the wrong thing. So if you're tempted to misbehave when nobody is looking, remember this: There is never a time when "nobody's watching." Somebody is always watching over you—and that Somebody, of course, is your Father in Heaven. Don't let Him down!

Kid's Tip: When it comes to telling the world about your relationship with God . . . your actions speak much more loudly than your words . . . so behave accordingly.

The Right Choice

But Daniel purposed in his heart that
he would not defile himself . . . .

Daniel 1:8 KJV

Your life is a series of choices. From the instant
you wake up in the morning until the moment you
nod off to sleep at night, you make lots of decisions:
decisions about the things you do, decisions about
the words you speak, and decisions about the
thoughts you choose to think.

So, if you want to lead a life that is pleasing to
God, you must make choices that are pleasing to
Him. And you know what? He deserves no less . . .
and neither, for that matter, do you.

Kid's Tip: When you make wise choices . . . You make
everybody happy. You make your parents happy, you
make your teachers happy, you make your friends
happy, and you make God happy!

Try to Memorize This Verse

**I have learned to be content
in whatever circumstances I am.**

Philippians 4:11 Holman CSB

This is an important Bible verse.
Practice saying it several times. And then, talk to
mom or dad about exactly what the verse means . . .

A Tip for Parents: Talk to your child about . . .

True contentment

Good and Evil

Friend, don't go along with evil. Model the good.
The person who does good does God's work.
The person who does evil falsifies God,
doesn't know the first thing about God.

3 John 1:11 MSG

When other people are unkind, you may be
tempted to strike back in anger. But God
doesn't want you to fight your way through life! God
wants you to forgive other people, even when they
haven't behaved themselves, even when they've
been very mean. So, when other people aren't nice,
forgive them as quickly as you can. And let God take
care of everything else.

God shapes the world by prayer. The more praying
there is in the world, the better the world will be,
and the mightier will be the forces against evil.

E. M. Bounds

Being a Good Example to Your Friends

We have around us many people whose lives tell us what faith means. So let us run the race that is before us and never give up. We should remove from our lives anything that would get in the way and the sin that so easily holds us back.

Hebrews 12:1 NCV

A re you a person whose behavior serves as a good example for other kids? If so, congratulations! God smiles upon people (like you) who do what's right, but that's not all. God also rewards good behavior when He sees it (and you can be sure that He sees it!).

So do yourself and your friends a favor: Do the right thing every chance you get.

Kid's Tip: As an example for living, look to Jesus.

Respecting Others

Just as you want others to do for you,
do the same for them.

Luke 6:31 Holman CSB

How should you treat other people? Jesus has the answer to that question. Jesus wants you to treat other people exactly like you want to be treated: with kindness, respect, and courtesy. When you do, you'll make your family and friends happy . . . and that's what God wants.

So if you're wondering how to treat someone else, follow the Golden Rule: treat the other people like you want them to treat you. When you do, you'll be obeying your Father in heaven and you'll be making other folks happy at the same time.

Kid's Tip: When dealing with other people, it is important to try to "walk in their shoes."

Changing Habits

Do not be deceived:
"Evil company corrupts good habits."
1 Corinthians 15:33 NKJV

Most people have a few habits they'd like to change, and maybe you do, too. If so, God can help.

If you trust God, and if you keep asking Him to help you change bad habits, He will help you make yourself into a new person. So, if at first you don't succeed, keep praying. God is listening, and He's ready to help you a better person if you ask Him . . . so ask Him!

Kid's Tip: The Importance of Having Healthy Habits: the old saying is familiar and true: "First you make your habits; then your habits make you." So it's always a good time to ask this question: "What kind of person are my habits making me?"

Questions?

An indecisive man is unstable in all his ways.
James 1:8 Holman CSB

God doesn't explain Himself to us with the clarity that we humans would prefer (think about this: if God did explain Himself with perfect clarity, we wouldn't have enough brainpower to understand the explanation that He gave!)

When innocent people are hurt, we question God because we can't figure out exactly what He's doing, or why. Since we can't fully answer that question now, we must trust in God's love, God's wisdom, and God's plan.

And while we're waiting for that wonderful day when all our questions will be answered (in heaven), we should use the time that we have here on earth to help the people who need it most.

Kid's Tip: Got Questions? If you're faced with too many questions and too few answers, slow down, and talk to your parents. When you do, you'll discover that your patents probably have more answers than you have questions.

Sometimes Sad

Those people who know they have great spiritual needs are happy, because the kingdom of heaven belongs to them. Those who are sad now are happy, because God will comfort them.

Matthew 5:3-4 NCV

Sometimes, you feel happy, and sometimes you don't. When you're feeling sad, here are two very important things you should do: 1. Talk to your parents about your feelings. 2. Talk to God about your feelings.

Talking with your parents is helpful because your mom and dad understand this: The problems that seem VERY BIG to you today probably won't seem so big tomorrow.

Talking with God helps because God hears your prayers and He helps make things better.

So the next time you're sad, don't hold your feelings inside—talk things over with your parents and with God. When you do, you'll feel better . . . and so will they!

God is good, and heaven is forever. These two facts should brighten up even the darkest day.

Marie T. Freeman

Keep On Forgiving

You have heard that it was said, "Love your neighbor
and hate your enemies." But I say to you,
love your enemies. Pray for those who hurt you.

Matthew 5:43–44 NCV

If you forgive somebody once, that's enough,
right? WRONG!!! Even if you've forgiven
somebody many times before, you must keep on
forgiving.

Jesus teaches us that we must keep forgiving
people even if they continue to misbehave. Why?
Because we, too, need to be forgiven over and over
again. And if God keeps forgiving us, then we must
be willing to do the same thing for others.

If Jesus forgave those who nailed Him to
the Cross, and if God forgives you and me,
how can you withhold your forgiveness
from someone else?

Anne Graham Lotz

Friends You Can Trust

Friends come and friends go,
but a true friend sticks by you like family.

Proverbs 18:24 MSG

All lasting friendships are built upon both honesty and trust. Without trust, friends soon drift apart. But with trust, friends can stay friends for a lifetime.

As Christians, we should always try to be trustworthy friends. And, we should be thankful for the people who are loyal friends to us. When we treat other people with honesty and respect, we not only make more friends, but we also keep the friendships we've already made.

Do you want friends you can trust? Then start by being a friend they can trust. That's the way to make your friendships strong, stronger, and strongest!

Kid's Tip: You make friends by being a friend. And when you choose your friends, choose wisely.

Love to Share

And we have known and believed the love that
God has for us. God is love, and he who abides in
love abides in God, and God in him.

1 John 4:16 NKJV

The Bible tells us that God is love and that if
we wish to know Him, we must have love in our
hearts. Sometimes, of course, when we're tired,
angry, or frustrated, it is very hard for us to be
loving. Thankfully, anger and frustration are feelings
that come and go, but God's love lasts forever.

If you'd like to improve your day and your life,
share God's love with your family and friends. Every
time you love, and every time you give, God smiles.

Kid's Tip: God's Love Is Our Greatest Security
Blanket: Kay Arthur's advises, "Snuggle in God's
arms. When you are hurting, when you feel lonely or
left out, let Him cradle you, comfort you, reassure
you of His all-sufficient power and love." Enough
said.

Patiently Waiting

We can make our plans,
but the LORD determines our steps.

Proverbs 16:9 NLT

God has a plan for you. But God's plan may not always happen in the way that you would like or at the time of your own choosing. Still, God always knows best.

Sometimes, even though you may want something very badly, you must still be patient and wait for the right time to get it, And the right time, of course, is determined by God. So trust Him always, obey Him always, and wait for Him to show you His plans. And that's exactly what He will do.

Kid's Tip: Your Plans, Or God's Plans? As you plan for this day and for all the ones that follow it, you should do so in prayerful consultation with your Father in heaven.

Being a Good Samaritan

Never walk away from someone who deserves help;
your hand is God's hand for that person.
Proverbs 3:27 MSG

Sometimes we would like to help make the world a better place, but we're not sure how to do it. Jesus told the story of the "Good Samaritan," a man who helped a fellow traveler when no one else would. We, too, should be good Samaritans when we find people who need our help. A good place to start helping other people is at home. And of course, we should also offer our help at school and at church.

Another way that we can help other people is to pray for them. God always hears our prayers, so we should talk with Him as often as we can. When we do, we're not only doing a wonderful thing for the people we pray for, we're also doing a wonderful thing for ourselves, too. Why? Because we feel better about ourselves when we're helping other people. And the more we help others, the better we should feel about ourselves.

Kid's Tip: If you can, help.

Look Before You Leap

Enthusiasm without knowledge is not good.
If you act too quickly, you might make a mistake.
Proverbs 19:2 NCV

Are you sometimes just a little bit impulsive? Do you sometimes fail to look before you leap? If so, God wants you to be a little bit more careful—or maybe a lot more careful!

The Bible makes it clear: we're supposed to behave wisely, not carelessly. But sometimes we're tempted to rush ahead and do things before we think about them.

So do yourself a big favor—slow down, think things through, and look carefully before you leap.

Kid's Tip: Not so fast! If you're about to do something, but you're not sure if it's the right thing to do, slow down! It's better to make a good decision than a fast decision.

Don't Judge!

Don't pick on people, jump on their failures,
criticize their faults—unless, of course,
you want the same treatment.
That critical spirit has a way of boomeranging.

Matthew 7:1-2 MSG

Here's something worth thinking about: If you judge other people harshly, God will judge you in the same way. But that's not all (thank goodness!) The Bible also promises that if you forgive other people, you, too, will be forgiven.

Are you tempted to blame people, criticize people, or judge people? If so, remember this: God is already judging what people do, and He doesn't need—or want—your help.

Kid's Tip: The ability to judge others requires a divine insight that you simply don't have.

Day 245

Be a Good Listener

My dearly loved brothers,
understand this: everyone must be quick to hear,
slow to speak, and slow to anger.

James 1:19 Holman CSB

When God made you, he gave you two ears and one mouth for a very good reason: you can learn at least twice as much by listening as you can by talking. That's why it's usually better to listen first and talk second. But when you're frustrated or tired, it's easy to speak first and think later.

A big part of growing up is learning how to slow down long enough to listen to the things that people have to say. So the next time you're tempted to turn off your ears and tune up your mouth, stop, listen, and think. After all, God gave you two wonderful ears for a very good reason: to use them.

Kid's Tip: Try to listen as much (or more) than you speak.

Today's Ideas About Prayer

Here are two important ideas. Take a few minutes to talk to your mom or dad about what these quotations mean.

Don't be overwhelmed . . .
take it one day and one prayer at a time.

Stormie Omartian

Just as our faith strengthens
our prayer life, so do our prayers
deepen our faith. Let us pray often,
starting today, for a deeper,
more powerful faith.

Shirley Dobson

Obeying Your Parents

We must obey God rather than men.

Acts 5:29 NASB

When your parents ask you to do something, do you usually obey them or do you usually ignore them? When your parents try to get your attention, do you listen or not? When your parents make rules, do you obey those rules or do you break them? Hopefully, you've learned to listen to your parents and to obey.

In order to be an obedient person, you must first learn how to control yourself—otherwise, you won't be able to behave yourself even if you want to. Controlling yourself means that you must slow down long enough to listen to your parents, and then you must be willing to do something about the things your parents tell you to do.

When you learn the importance of obedience, you'll soon discover that good things happen when you behave yourself. And the sooner you learn to listen and to obey, the sooner those good things will start happening . . . to you!

Anger Leads to Trouble

Patience is better than strength.
Proverbs 16:32 ICB

In the Book of Proverbs, King Solomon gave us wonderful advice for living wisely. Solomon warned that impatience and anger lead only to trouble. And he was right!

The next time you're tempted to say an unkind word or to throw a temper tantrum, remember Solomon. He was one of the wisest men who ever lived, and he knew that it's always better to be patient. So remain calm and remember that patience is best. After all, if it's good enough for a wise man like Solomon, it should be good enough for us, too.

Kid's Tip: God and your parents have been patient with you . . . now it's your turn to be patient with others.

Pleasing God!

For am I now trying to win the favor of people,
or God? Or am I striving to please people?
If I were still trying to please people,
I would not be a slave of Christ.

Galatians 1:10 Holman CSB

Are you a people-pleaser or a God-pleaser?
Hopefully, you're far more concerned with
pleasing God than you are with pleasing your friends.
But face facts: even if you're a devoted Christian,
you're still going to feel the urge to impress your
friends—and sometimes that urge will be strong.

Here's your choice: you can choose to please God
first, or you can fall victim to peer pressure. The
choice is yours—and so are the consequences.

Kid's Tip: Make up your mind to hang out with
people who will put pressure on you to become a
better person.

Making Things Better

For out of the overflow of the heart
the mouth speaks.

Matthew 12:34 NIV

When we're frustrated or tired, it's easier to speak first and think second. But that's not the best way to talk to other people. The Bible tells us that "a good person's words will help many others." But if our words are to be helpful, we must put some thought into them.

The next time you're tempted to say something unkind, remember that your words can and should be helpful to others, not hurtful. God wants to use you to make this world a better place, and He will use the things that you say to help accomplish that goal . . . if you let Him.

Kid's Tip: Words have immense power to encourage or discourage others.

Try to Memorize This Verse

**For to me to live is Christ,
and to die is gain.**

Philippians 1:21 KJV

This is an important Bible verse.
Practice saying it several times. And then, talk to
mom or dad about exactly what the verse means . . .

A Tip for Parents: Talk to your child about . . .

Living for Christ

The Courage to Tell the Truth

And you shall know the truth,
and the truth shall make you free.

John 8:32 NKJV

Sometimes, we're afraid of what might happen if we tell the truth. And sometimes, instead of doing the courageous thing, we do the unwise thing: we lie.

When we're fearful, we can and should find strength from friends, from family members and from God.

So if you're afraid to tell the truth, don't be! Keep looking until you find the courage to be honest. Then, you'll discover it's not the truth that you should be afraid of; it's those troublesome, pesky lies!

Only Jesus Christ is the truth for everyone who has ever been born into the human race, regardless of culture, age, nationality, generation, heritage, gender, color, or language.

Anne Graham Lotz

It's Easy to Worry

The Lord himself will go before you.
He will be with you; he will not leave you or
forget you. Don't be afraid and don't worry.

Deuteronomy 31:8 NCV

It's easy to worry about things—big things and little things. But the Bible promises us that if we learn to trust God more and more each day, we won't worry so much.

Are you worried about something? If so, try doing these two things: first, ask God for His help. And second, talk things over with your parents. When you do these things, you won't worry so much. And that's good . . . VERY good!

Kid's Tip: Worried about something you said or did? If you made a mistake yesterday, the day to fix it is today. Then, you won't have to worry about it tomorrow.

Stop and Think

Now you must rid yourselves of all such things as
these: anger, rage, malice . . . .

Colossians 3:8 NIV

When we lose control of our emotions, we do things that we shouldn't do. Sometimes, we throw tantrums. How silly! Other times we pout or whine. Too bad!

The Bible tells us that it is foolish to become angry and that it is wise to remain calm. That's why we should learn to slow down and think about things before we do them.

Do you want to make life better for yourself and for your family? Then be patient and think things through. Stop and think before you do things, not after. It's the wise thing to do.

Kid's Tip: Think carefully . . . make that very carefully! If you're a little angry, think carefully before you speak. If you're very angry, think very carefully. Otherwise, you might say something in anger that you'll regret later.

God Wrote a Book

For I am not ashamed of the gospel, because it is God's power for salvation to everyone who believes.

Romans 1:16 Holman CSB

If you want to know God, you should read the book He wrote. It's called the Bible (of course!), and God uses it to teach you and guide you. The Bible is not like any other book. It is an amazing gift from your Heavenly Father.

D. L. Moody observed, "The Bible was not given to increase our knowledge but to change our lives." God's Holy Word is, indeed, a life-changing, one-of-a-kind treasure. Handle it with care, but more importantly, handle it every day!

Kid's Tip: Learning about Jesus: Start learning about Jesus, and keep learning about Him as long as you live. His story never grows old, and His teachings never fail.

A Cheerful Heart

Jacob said, "For what a relief it is to see your
friendly smile. It is like seeing the smile of God!"
Genesis 33:10 NLT

The Bible tells us that a cheerful heart is like
medicine: it makes us feel better. Where does
cheerfulness begin? It begins inside each of us; it
begins in the heart. So let's be thankful to God for
His blessings, and let's show our thanks by sharing
good cheer wherever we go.

Today, make sure that you share a smile and a
kind word with as many people as you can. This old
world needs all the cheering up it can get . . . and so
do your friends.

Kid's Tip: Cheer up somebody else. Do you need
a little cheering up? If so, find somebody else
who needs cheering up, too. Then, do your best
to brighten that person's day. When you do,
you'll discover that cheering up other people is a
wonderful way to cheer yourself up, too!

Try to Memorize This Verse

I can do all things through Christ which strengtheneth me.

Philippians 4:13 KJV

This is an important Bible verse.
Practice saying it several times. And then, talk to mom or dad about exactly what the verse means . . .

A Tip for Parents: Talk to your child about . . .

The strength Christ gives

Encourage Each Other

So encourage each other and give each
other strength, just as you are doing now.

1 Thessalonians 5:11 NCV

When other people are sad, what can we do? We
can do our best to cheer them up by showing
kindness and love.

The Bible tells us that we must care for each
other, and when everybody is happy, that's an easy
thing to do. But, when people are sad, for whatever
reason, it's up to us to speak a kind word or to offer
a helping hand.

Do you know someone who is discouraged or sad?
If so, perhaps it's time to take matters into your
own hands. Think of something you can do to cheer
that person up . . . and then do it! You'll make two
people happy.

Kid's Tip: Do you want to be successful and go far in
life? Encourage others to do the same. You can't lift
other people up without lifting yourself up, too.

The Best Excuse Is No Excuse

The one who plants and the one who waters
have the same purpose, and each will be
rewarded for his own work.

1 Corinthians 3:8 NCV

What is an excuse? Well, when you make up an excuse, that means that you try to come up with a good reason that you didn't do something that you should have done.

Anybody can make up excuses, and you can too. But you shouldn't get into the habit of making too many excuses. Why? Because excuses don't work. And why don't they work? Because everybody has already heard so many excuses that almost everybody can recognize excuses when they hear them.

So the next time you're tempted to make up an excuse, don't. Instead of making an excuse, do what you think is right. After all, the very best excuse of all . . . is no excuse.

Making up a string of excuses is usually harder
than doing the work.

Marie T. Freeman

Forgive . . . Quickly

Be even-tempered, content with second place, quick
to forgive an offense. Forgive as quickly
and completely as the Master forgave you.
And regardless of what else you put on,
wear love. It's your basic, all-purpose garment.
Never be without it.

Colossians 3:13-14 MSG

When you make a mistake or hurt someone's feelings, what should you do? You should say you're sorry and ask for forgiveness. And you should do so sooner, not later.

The longer you wait to apologize, the harder it is on you. So if you've done something wrong, don't be afraid to ask for forgiveness, and don't be afraid to ask for it NOW!

Kid's Tip: Forgiving other people is one way of strengthening your relationship with God . . .

Friends Are a Good Thing

If you've gotten anything at all out of following
Christ, if his love has made any difference in your
life, if being in a community of the Spirit means
anything to you, if you have a heart, if you care—
then do me a favor: Agree with each other,
love each other, be deep-spirited friends.

Philippians 2:1-2 MSG

The Bible tells us that friendship can be a
wonderful thing. That's why it's good to know
how to make and to keep good friends.

If you want to make lots of friends, practice
the Golden Rule with everybody you know. Be kind.
Share. Say nice things. Be helpful. When you do,
you'll discover that the Golden Rule isn't just a nice
way to behave; it's also a great way to make and to
keep friends!

Kid's Tip: If you want to make more friends,
how can you do it? Try this: First, become more
interested in them . . . and pretty soon they'll
become more interested in you!

Try to Memorize This Verse

Where the Spirit of the Lord is, there is freedom.

2 Corinthians 3:17 NIV

This is an important Bible verse.
Practice saying it several times. And then, talk to
mom or dad about exactly what the verse means . . .

A Tip for Parents: Talk to your child about . . .

True freedom

Learning to Be More Obedient

Here is my final advice: Honor God
and obey his commands.
Ecclesiastes 12:13 ICB

Learning how to control yourself helps you become a more obedient person. So the more you learn about self-control, the better.

Learning how to control yourself is a good thing. Self-control helps you at home, at school, and at church. That's why parents and teachers are happy to talk about the rewards of good behavior.

If you want to learn more about self-control, ask your parents. They'll help you figure out better ways to behave yourself. And that's good for everybody . . . especially you!

Kid's Tip: Be patient, and follow the rules . . . even if you don't like some of the rules that you're supposed to follow, follow them anyway.

Doing the Right Thing

The honest person will live safely,
but the one who is dishonest will be caught.
Proverbs 10:9 ICB

Nobody can tell the truth for you. You're the one who decides what you are going to say. You're the one who decides whether your words will be truthful . . . or not.

The word "integrity" means doing the right and honest thing. If you're going to be a person of integrity, it's up to you. If you want to live a life that is pleasing to God and to others, make integrity a habit. When you do, everybody wins, especially you!

Kid's Tip: Honesty, Honesty, Honesty: Unless you build your relationships on honesty, you're building on a slippery, sandy slope.

Getting to Know Him

If your life honors the name of Jesus,
he will honor you.
2 Thessalonians 1:12 MSG

There's really no way around it: If you want to know God, you need to know His Son. And that's good, because getting to know Jesus can—and should—be a wonderful experience.

Jesus has an amazing love for you, so welcome Him into your heart today. When you do, you'll always be grateful that you did.

Not the goods of the world, but God.
Not riches, but God. Not honors, but God.
Not advancement, but God.
God always and in everything.
Vincent Pallotti

Kid's Tip: Do you want them to follow in the footsteps of Jesus? Then you must lead the way. Actions speak louder than sermons . . . much louder.

Forgive and Forget

And forgive us our sins, for we ourselves also
forgive everyone in debt to us.

Luke 11:4 Holman CSB

Have you heard the saying, "Forgive and forget"?
Well, it's certainly easier said than done. It's
easy to talk about forgiving somebody, but actually
forgiving that person can be much harder to do. And
when it comes to forgetting, forget about it!

Sometimes, it's impossible to forget the people
who hurt our feelings. But even if we can't forget,
we can forgive. And that's exactly what God teaches
us to do.

Kid's Tip: Forgive . . . and keep forgiving!
Sometimes, you may forgive someone once and then,
at a later time, become angry at the very same
person again. If so, you must forgive that person
again and again
. . . until it sticks!

Good Friends Behave

As iron sharpens iron,
so people can improve each other.

Proverbs 27:17 NCV

Our world is filled with pressures: some good, some bad. The pressures that we feel to follow God's rules are the good kind of pressures (and the friends who make us want to obey God are good friends). But sometimes, we may feel pressure to misbehave, pressure from friends who want us to disobey the rules.

If you want to please God and your parents, make friends with people who behave themselves. When you do, you'll be much more likely to behave yourself, too . . . and that's a very good thing.

Kid's Tip: If you choose friends who behave themselves . . . you'll be far more likely to behave yourself, too.

Share Your Blessings

Remember this: the person who sows sparingly will also reap sparingly, and the person who sows generously will also reap generously.

2 Corinthians 9:6 Holman CSB

Jesus told us that we should be generous with other people, but sometimes we don't feel much like sharing. Instead of sharing the things that we have, we want to keep them all to ourselves. But God doesn't want selfishness to rule our hearts; He wants us to be generous.

Are you lucky enough to have nice things? If so, God's instructions are clear: you must share your blessings with others. And that's exactly the way it should be. After all, think how generous God has been with you.

Kid's Tip: There is a direct relationship between generosity and joy—the more you give to others, the more joy you will experience for yourself.

Never-ending Love

The unfailing love of the Lord never ends!
Lamentations 3:22 NLT

How much does God love you? He loves you so much that He sent His Son Jesus to come to this earth for you! And, when you accept Jesus into your heart, God gives you a gift that is more precious than gold: that gift is called "eternal life" which means that you will live forever with God in heaven!

God's love is bigger and more powerful than anybody can imagine, but it is very real. So do yourself a favor right now: accept God's love with open arms and welcome His Son Jesus into your heart. When you do, your life will be changed today, tomorrow, and forever.

As God's children, we are the recipients of lavish love—a love that motivates us to keep trusting even when we have no idea what God is doing.
Beth Moore

Today's Ideas About
Wisdom

Here are two important ideas. Take a few minutes to talk to your mom or dad about what these quotations mean.

If you lack knowledge, go to school.
If you lack wisdom, get on your knees.

Vance Havner

You may as well quit reading
and hearing the Word of God and give it
to the devil if you do not desire
to live according to it.

Martin Luther

Is the Golden Rule Your Rule, Too?

When you do things, do not let selfishness or pride be your guide. Instead, be humble and give more honor to others than to yourselves.

Philippians 2:3 NCV

Is the Golden Rule your rule, or is it just another Bible verse that goes in one ear and out the other? Jesus made Himself perfectly clear: He instructed you to treat other people in the same way that you want to be treated. But sometimes, especially when you're feeling pressure from friends, or when we're tired or upset, obeying the Golden Rule can seem like an impossible task—but it's not. So be kind to everybody and obey God's rule, the Golden Rule, that is.

Kid's Tip: You must do more than talk about it: In order to be a good person, you must do good things. So get busy! The best time to do a good deed is as soon as you can do it!

The Habit of Honesty

Those who want to do right more than anything else
are happy. God will fully satisfy them.
Matthew 5:6 ICB

Our lives are made up of lots and lots of habits.
And the habits we choose help determine the
kind of people we become. If we choose habits that
are good, we are happier and healthier. If we choose
habits that are bad, then it's too bad for us!

Honesty, like so many other things, is a habit.
And it's a habit that is right for you.

Do you want to grow up to become the kind of
person that God intends for you to be? Then get
into the habit of being honest with everybody. You'll
be glad you did . . . and so will God!

If you want to form a new habit, get to work.
If you want to break a bad habit,
get on your knees.
Marie T. Freeman

White Lies?

Doing what is right brings freedom to honest people.

Proverbs 11:6 ICB

Sometimes, people convince themselves that it's okay to tell "little white lies." Sometimes people convince themselves that itsy bitsy lies aren't harmful. But there's a problem: little lies have a way of growing into big ones, and once they grow up, they cause lots of problems.

Remember that lies, no matter what size, are not part of God's plan for our lives, so tell the truth about everything. It's the right thing to do, and besides: when you always tell the truth, you don't have to try and remember what you said!

The single most important element in any human relationship is honesty—with oneself, with God, and with others.

Catherine Marshall

A Fruitful Friendship

I am the Vine, you are the branches. When you're joined with me and I with you, the relation intimate and organic, the harvest is sure to be abundant.

John 15:5 MSG

Whether you realize it or not, you already have a relationship with Jesus. Hopefully, it's a close relationship! Why? Because the friendship you form with Jesus will help you every day of your life . . . and beyond!

You can either choose to invite Him into your heart, or you can ignore Him altogether. Welcome Him today—and while you're at it, encourage your friends and family members to do the same.

I am truly happy with Jesus Christ. I couldn't live without Him. When my life gets beyond the ability to cope, He takes over.

Ruth Bell Graham

Laughter Is a Gift

There is a time for everything,
and everything on earth has its special season. . . .
There is a time to cry and a time to laugh.
There is a time to be sad and a time to dance.

Ecclesiastes 3:1,4 NCV

Do you like to laugh? Of course you do! Laughter is a gift from God that He hopes you'll use in the right way. So here are a few things to remember:

1. God wants you to be happy. 2. Laughter is a good thing when you're laughing at the right things. 3. You should laugh with people, but you should never laugh at them.

God created laughter for a reason . . . and God knows best. So do yourself a favor: laugh at the right things . . . and laugh a lot!

Kid's Tip: Learn to laugh at life: Life has a lighter side—look for it, especially when times are tough. Laughter is medicine for the soul, so take your medicine early and often.

Today's Ideas About
Going to Church

Here are two important ideas. Take a few minutes to talk to your mom or dad about what these quotations mean.

The church needs people who are doers of the Word and not just hearers.

Warren Wiersbe

The Bible knows nothing of solitary religion.

John Wesley

Obey Your Teachers

And the world with its lust is passing away,
but the one who does God's will remains forever.

1 John 2:17 Holman CSB

It's good to obey your teachers, but before you can obey them, you must make sure you understand what your teachers are saying. So, in order to be an obedient student, you must be a student who knows how to listen.

Once you decide to be a careful listener, you'll become a better learner, too. But if you're determined to talk to other kids while your teachers are teaching, you won't learn very much.

So do yourself a favor: when you go to school, listen and obey. You'll be glad you did. . . and your teachers will be glad, too.

Kid's Tip: Learning how to obey makes you a better person. You have many teachers. Listen to them and obey them. When you do, you'll become a better person.

Hopes, Hopes, and More Hopes

Make me hear joy and gladness.
Psalm 51:8 NKJV

Hope is a very good thing to have . . . and to share. So make this promise to yourself and keep it: promise yourself that you'll be a hopeful person. Think good thoughts. Trust God. Become friends with Jesus. And trust your hopes, not your fears. Then, when you've filled your heart with hope and gladness, share your good thoughts with friends. They'll be better for it, and so will you.

Kid's Tip: Think about all the things you have (starting with your family and your faith) . . . and think about all the things you can do! Believe in yourself.

Peace of Mind

I leave you peace. My peace I give you.
I do not give it to you as the world does.
So don't let your hearts be troubled.
John 14:27 ICB

Patience and peace go together. And the words from John 14:27 remind us that Jesus offers us peace, not as the world gives, but as He alone gives. We, as believers, can accept His peace or ignore it. When we accept the peace of Jesus Christ into our hearts, our lives are changed forever, and we become more loving, patient Christians.

Christ's peace is offered freely; it has already been paid for; it is ours for the asking. So let us ask . . . and then share.

You're in a hurry. God is not. Trust God.
Marie T. Freeman

Staying Out of Trouble

Don't envy bad people; don't even want to be around them. All they think about is causing a disturbance; all they talk about is making trouble.

Proverbs 24:1-2 MSG

One way that you can feel better about yourself is by staying out of trouble. And one way that you can stay out of trouble is by making friends with people who, like you, want to do what's right.

Are your friends the kind of kids who encourage you to behave yourself? If so, you've chosen your friends wisely. But if your friends try to get you in trouble, perhaps it's time to think long and hard about making some new friends.

Whether you know it or not, you're probably going to behave like your friends behave. So pick out friends who make you want to behave better, not worse. When you do, you'll feel better about yourself . . . a whole lot better.

For better or worse, you will eventually become more and more like the people you associate with. So why not associate with people who make you better, not worse?

Marie T. Freeman

Today's Ideas About
God's Love

Here are two important ideas. Take a few minutes to talk to your mom or dad about what these quotations mean.

The Bible has a simple story.
God made man. Man rejected God.
God won't give up until he wins him back.
Max Lucado

The love of God is revealed in that
He laid down His life for His enemies.
Oswald Chambers

The Very Best Time to Forgive Somebody Is Now

Working together with Him, we also appeal to you:
"Don't receive God's grace in vain." For He says:
In an acceptable time, I heard you, and in the day of
salvation, I helped you. Look, now is the acceptable
time; look, now is the day of salvation.

2 Corinthians 6:1-2 Holman CSB

When is the best time to forgive somebody? Well, as the old saying goes, there's no time like the present. So if you have somebody you need to forgive, why not forgive that person today?

Forgiving other people is one of the ways that we make ourselves feel better. So if you're still angry about something that somebody did, forgive that person right now. There is no better time.

Kid's Tip: When the Lord tells you it is time to do something (like forgive someone), the time to do it is now.

Let's Be Patient

Knowledge begins with respect for the Lord, but
fools hate wisdom and self-control.
Proverbs 1:7 NCV

The Bible tells us that we should be patient with
everybody, not just with parents, teachers,
and friends. In the eyes of God, all people are very
important, so we should treat them that way.

Of course it's easy to be nice to the people we
want to impress, but what about everybody else?
Jesus gave us clear instructions: He said that when
we do a good deed for someone less fortunate
than we are, we have also done a good deed for our
Savior. And as Christians, that's exactly what we
are supposed to do!

Kid's Tip: Speak respectfully to everybody, starting
with parents, grandparents, teachers, and adults . . .
but don't stop there. Be respectful of everybody,
including yourself!

Yes, Jesus Loves You!

You're blessed when you're content with just who you are—no more, no less. That's the moment you find yourselves proud owners of everything that can't be bought.

Matthew 5:5 MSG

Have you heard the song "Jesus Loves Me"? Probably so. It's a happy song that should remind you of this important fact: Jesus loves you very much.

When you invite Jesus into your heart, He will be your friend forever. If you make mistakes, He'll still be your friend. When you aren't perfect, He'll still love you. If you feel sorry or sad, He can help you feel better.

Yes, Jesus loves you . . . and you should love yourself. So the next time you feel sad about yourself . . . or something that you've done . . . remember that Jesus loves you, your family loves you, and you should feel that way, too.

Kid's Tip: There's only one you! Nobody else in the world is exactly like you. When God made you, He made a very special, one-of-a-kind person.

Friends Should Share

The righteous give without sparing.

Proverbs 21:26 NIV

How can you be a good friend? One way is by sharing. And here are some of the things you can share: smiles, kind words, pats on the back, your toys, school supplies, books, and, of course, your prayers.

Would you like to make your friends happy? And would you like to make yourself happy at the same time? Here's how: treat your friends like you want to be treated. That means obeying the Golden Rule, which, of course, means sharing. In fact, the more you share, the better friend you'll be.

Kid's Tip: Sharing with guests is an important way to demonstrate hospitality.

Martha and Mary

But Martha was pulled away by all she had to do in the kitchen. Later, she stepped in, interrupting them. "Master, don't you care that my sister has abandoned the kitchen to me? Tell her to lend me a hand." The Master said, "Martha, dear Martha, you're fussing far too much and getting yourself worked up over nothing. One thing only is essential, and Mary has chosen it - it's the main course, and won't be taken from her."

Luke 10:40-42 MSG

Okay, after that rather long Bible passage, your devotional is almost up, so we'll make it short and sweet: Martha was concerned with doing things for Jesus. Mary was concerned with being with Jesus. Mary made the better choice. Why? Because we need to be with Christ before we start doing things for Him. End of lesson.

When we are in a situation where Jesus is all we have, we soon discover he is all we really need.

Gigi Graham Tchividjian

Try to Memorize This Verse

"And they shall call His name Immanuel,"
which is translated, "God with us."
Matthew 1:23 NKJV

This is an important Bible verse.
Practice saying it several times. And then, talk to
mom or dad about exactly what the verse means . . .

A Tip for Parents: Talk to your child about . . .

"God with us"

Think About the Other Person

I pray that your love for each other will
overflow more and more, and that you will
keep on growing in your knowledge
and understanding.

Philippians 1:9 NLT

There's an old saying that goes something like
this: "Try to put yourself in the other person's
shoes." It means that the more you understand
somebody, the easier it is to forgive that person.

When you become angry with someone, try
putting yourself in the other person's shoes.
When you do, perhaps you'll be a little bit more
understanding—and a little bit quicker to forgive.

Kid's Tip: It is important for you to be
understanding to your friends and family.

Try to Memorize This Verse

And remember, I am with you always,
to the end of the age.
Matthew 28:20 Holman CSB

This is an important Bible verse.
Practice saying it several times. And then, talk to
mom or dad about exactly what the verse means . . .

A Tip for Parents: Talk to your child about . . .

God's closeness

About Barnabas

Barnabas was a good man, full of the Holy Spirit
and full of faith.
Acts 11:23-24 ICB

Barnabas was a leader in the early Christian
church who was known for his kindness and
for his ability to encourage others. Because of
Barnabas, many people were introduced to Christ.

We become like Barnabas when we speak kind
words to our families and to our friends. And then,
because we have been generous and kind, the people
around us can see how Christians should behave. So
when in doubt, be kind and generous to others, just
like Barnabas.

Kid's Tip: Be an Encourager! Barnabas was known as
a man who encouraged others. In other words, he
made other people feel better by saying kind things.
You, like Barnabas, can encourage your family and
friends . . . and you should.

Avoiding Mischief

Therefore as you have received Christ Jesus
the Lord, walk in Him.

Colossians 2:6 Holman CSB

Face facts: not everybody you know is well behaved. Your first job is to recognize bad behavior when you see it . . . and your second job is to make sure that you don't join in!

The moment that you decide to avoid mischief whenever you see it is the moment that you'll make yourself happy, your parents happy, and God happy. And you'll stay out of trouble. And you'll be glad you did!

Christians are the citizens of heaven,
and while we are on earth, we ought to behave
like heaven's citizens.

Warren Wiersbe

A Wise Man

If you need wisdom—if you want to know what God wants you to do—ask him, and he will gladly tell you. He will not resent your asking.

James 1:5 NLT

Solomon wasn't just a king. He was also a very wise man and a very good writer. He even wrote several books in the Bible! So when He finally put down His pen, what was this wise man's final advice? It's simple: Solomon said: "Honor God and obey His commandments."

The next time you have an important choice to make, ask yourself this: "Am I honoring God and obeying Him? And am I doing what God wants me to do?" If you can answer those questions with a great big "YES," then go ahead. But if you're uncertain if the choice you are about to make is the right one, slow down. Why? Because that's what Solomon says . . . and that's what God says, too!

God is voting for us all the time.
The devil is voting against us all the time.
The way we vote carries the election.

Corrie ten Boom

Working Together

Work at getting along with each other and with God.
Otherwise you'll never get so much
as a glimpse of God.

Hebrews 12:14 MSG

Helping other people can be fun! When you help others, you feel better about yourself—and you'll know that God approves of what you're doing.

When you learn how to cooperate with your family and friends, you'll soon discover that it's more fun when everybody works together.

So do everybody a favor: learn better ways to share and better ways to cooperate. It's the right thing to do.

Kid's Tip: Cooperation pays: When you cooperate with your friends and family, you'll feel good about yourself—and your family and friends will feel good about you, too.

Difficult Days

We take the good days from God—
why not also the bad days?

Job 2:10 MSG

Face it: some days are better than others. But even on the days when you don't feel very good, God never leaves you for even a moment. So if you need assistance, you can always pray to God, knowing that He will listen and help.

If you're feeling unhappy, talk things over with God, and while you're at it, be sure and talk things over with your parents, too. And remember this: the sooner you start talking, the sooner things will get better.

When life is difficult, God wants us to have a faith that trusts and waits.

Kay Arthur

What Kind of Example?

You are young, but do not let anyone treat you as if
you were not important. Be an example to show
the believers how they should live. Show them with
your words, with the way you live, with your love,
with your faith, and with your pure life.

1 Timothy 4:12 ICB

Like it or not, your behavior is a powerful example
to others. The question is not whether you will
be an example to your friends; the only question is
this: What kind of example will you be?

Corrie ten Boom advised, "Don't worry about
what you do not understand. Worry about what you
do understand in the Bible but do not live by." And
that's good advice because your family and friends
are always watching . . . and so, for that matter, is
God.

Kid's Tip: Don't Exaggerate! All of us have enough
troubles without pretending that we have more.

Obeying God

Be gentle with one another, sensitive.
Forgive one another as quickly and thoroughly as
God in Christ forgave you.

Ephesians 4:32 MSG

How hard is it to forgive people? Sometimes, it's very hard! But God tells us that we must forgive other people, even when we'd rather not forgive them. So, if you're angry with anybody (or if you're upset by something you yourself have done) it's time to forgive.

God instructs us to treat other people exactly as we wish to be treated. When we forgive others, we are obeying our Heavenly Father, and that's exactly what we must try to do.

Kid's Tip: Forgiving other people is not necessarily the same as forgetting. Yet even when you cannot forget the past, you should try not to focus on the past.

Real Friends

A friend loves you all the time.
Proverbs 17:17 ICB

The Book of Proverbs tells us that true friends love us always. How wonderful that is! We should thank God for the family and friends He has brought into our lives.

Today, let's give thanks to God for all the people who love us, for brothers and sisters, parents and grandparents, aunts and uncles, cousins, and friends. And then, as a way of thanking God, let's obey Him by being especially kind to our loved ones. They deserve it, and so does He.

Kid's Tip: To grow your friendships, make the effort to spend time with your friends.

Day 298

Sharing and Self-esteem

God loves the person who gives happily.
2 Corinthians 9:7 ICB

Learning how to share can be an important way to build better self-esteem. Why? Because when you learn to share your things, you'll know that you've done exactly what God wants you to do—and you'll feel better about yourself.

The Bible teaches that it's better to be generous than selfish. But sometimes, you won't feel like sharing your things, and you'll be tempted to keep everything for yourself. When you're feeling a little bit stingy, remember this: God wants you to share your things with people who need your help.

When you learn to be a more generous person, God will be pleased with you . . . and you'll be pleased with yourself.

Kid's Tip: Generosity 101: Some of the best stuff you'll ever have is the stuff you give away.

Today's Ideas About God's Gifts

Here are two important ideas. Take a few minutes to talk to your mom or dad about what these quotations mean.

God gives His gifts where He finds the vessel empty enough to receive them.

C. S. Lewis

God is the giver, and we are the receivers. And His richest gifts are bestowed not upon those who do the greatest things, but upon those who accept His abundance and His grace.

Hannah Whitall Smith

Giving to Your Church

In everything I did, I showed you that by this kind
of hard work we must help the weak, remembering
the words the Lord Jesus himself said:
"It is more blessed to give than to receive."

Acts 20:35 NIV

When the offering plate passes by, are you old
enough to drop anything in it? If you are,
congratulations! But if you're not quite old enough
to give money to the church, don't worry—there are
still lots of things you can share!

Even when you don't have money to share, you
still have much to give to your church. What are
some things you can share? Well, you can share your
smile, your happiness, your laughter, your energy,
your cooperation, your prayers, your obedience, your
example, and your love.

So don't worry about giving to the church: even
if you don't have lots of money, there are still plenty
of ways you can give. And the best time to start
giving is NOW!

Kid's Tip: When other people need our help, we
should gladly share the things we have.

When You Don't Know What to Say

Watch the way you talk.
Let nothing foul or dirty come out of your mouth.
Say only what helps, each word a gift.
Ephesians 4:29 MSG

Sometimes, it's hard to know exactly what to say. And sometimes, it can be very tempting to say something that isn't true—or something that isn't nice. But when you say things you shouldn't say, you'll regret it later.

So make this promise to yourself, and keep it—promise to think about the things you say before you say them. And whatever you do, always tell the truth. When you do these things, you'll be doing yourself a big favor, and you'll be obeying the Word of God.

Kid's Tip: Think first, speak second: If you want to keep from hurting other people's feelings, don't open your mouth until you've turned on your brain.

Letting Other People Know What It Means to Be a Christian

But respect Christ as the holy Lord in your hearts. Always be ready to answer everyone who asks you to explain about the hope you have.

1 Peter 3:15 NCV

Every Christian, each in his or her own way, has a responsibility to share the Good News of our Jesus. And it's important to remember that we bear testimony through both words and actions. Wise Christians follow the advice of St. Francis of Assisi who advised, "Preach the gospel at all times and, if necessary, use words."

As you think about how your example influences others, remember that actions speak louder than words . . . much louder!

Kid's Tip: You share your testimony through words and actions.

The Truth

Go after a life of love as if your life depended on it—because it does. Give yourselves to the gifts God gives you. Most of all, try to proclaim his truth.

1 Corinthians 14:1 MSG

Jesus had a message for his followers. He said, "The truth will set you free." When we do the right thing and tell the truth, we don't need to worry about our lies catching up with us. When we behave honestly, we don't have to worry about feeling guilty or ashamed. But, if we fail to do what we know is right, bad things start to happen, and we feel guilty.

Jesus understood that the truth is a very good thing indeed. We should understand it, too. And we should keep telling it as long as we live.

Kid's Tip: Knowing the Truth . . . and Living It: Warren Wiersbe writes, " Learning God's truth and getting it into our heads is one thing, but living God's truth and getting it into our characters is quite something else." So don't be satisfied to sit on the sidelines and observe the truth at a distance— live it.

When We're Worried

Give all your worries and cares to God,
for he cares about what happens to you.
1 Peter 5:6 NLT

When we're worried, there are two places we should take our concerns: to the people who love and care for us and to God.

When troubles arise, it helps to talk about them with parents, grandparents, and concerned adults. But we shouldn't stop there: we should also talk to God through our prayers.

If you're worried about something, you can pray about it any time you want. And remember that God is always listening, and He always wants to hear from you.

So when you're worried, try this plan: talk and pray. Talk to the grownups who love you, and pray to the Heavenly Father who made you. The more you talk and the more you pray, the better you'll feel.

Kid's Tip: Troubles will pass more quickly if you spend more time solving problems and less time fretting over them.

Don't Whine!

Words kill, words give life;
they're either poison or fruit—you choose.

Proverbs 18:21 MSG

Do you like to listen to other children whine? No way! And since you don't like to hear other kids whining, then you certainly shouldn't whine, either.

Sometimes, kids think that whining is a good way to get the things they want . . . but it's not! So if your parents or your teacher ask you to do something, don't complain about it. And if there's something you want, don't whine and complain until you get it.

Remember: whining won't make you happy . . . and it won't make anybody else happy, either.

Kid's Tip: Whining can be contagious, so make sure that your home is, to the greatest extent possible, a whine-free zone. How can you do this? A good way to start is by counting your blessings, not your problems.

Because You're a Christian

Make the Master proud of you by being good citizens. Respect the authorities, whatever their level; they are God's emissaries for keeping order.

1 Peter 2:13-14 MSG

Do you behave differently because you're a Christian? Or do you behave in pretty much the same way that you would if you had never heard of Jesus? Hopefully, your behavior is better because of the things you've learned from the Bible.

Doing the right thing is not always easy, especially when you're tired or frustrated. But, doing the wrong thing almost always leads to trouble. So here's some advice: remember the lessons you learn from the Bible. And keep remembering them every day of your life.

Kid's Tip: If you're not sure that it's the right thing to do, don't do it! And if you're not sure that it's the truth, don't tell it.

Every Day Is a Special Day

David and the whole house of Israel were
celebrating before the Lord.

2 Samuel 6:5 Holman CSB

Today is a day of celebration, and hopefully, you do feel like celebrating! After all, today (like every other day) should be a special time to thank God for all the wonderful things He has given you.

So don't wait for birthdays or holidays—make every day a special day, including this one. Take time to pause and thank God for His gifts. He deserves your thanks, and you deserve to celebrate!

If you can forgive the person you were,
accept the person you are, and believe in
the person you will become, you are headed for joy.
So celebrate your life.

Barbara Johnson

That Little Voice

For God is pleased with you when,
for the sake of your conscience,
you patiently endure unfair treatment.

1 Peter 2:19 NLT

When you know that you're doing what's right, you'll feel better about yourself. Why? Because you have a little voice in your head called your "conscience." Your conscience is a feeling that tells you whether something is right or wrong—and it's a feeling that makes you feel better about yourself when you know you've done the right thing.

Your conscience is an important tool. Pay attention to it!

The more you listen to your conscience, the easier it is to behave yourself. So here's great advice: first, slow down long enough to figure out the right thing to do—and then do it! When you do, you'll be proud of yourself . . . and other people will be proud of you, too.

Kid's Tip: That tiny little voice inside your head . . . is called your conscience. Treat it like a trusted friend: Listen to the things it says; it's usually right!

When Things Go Wrong

But as for you, be strong; don't be discouraged,
for your work has a reward.

2 Chronicles 15:7 Holman CSB

Face facts: some days are more wonderful than other days. Sometimes, everything seems to go right, and on other days, many things seem to go wrong. But here's something to remember: even when you're disappointed with the way things turn out, God is near . . . and He loves you very much!

If you're disappointed, worried, sad, or afraid, you can talk to your parents and to God. And you certainly feel better when you do!

Often God has to shut a door in our face
so that he can subsequently open the door
through which he wants us to go.

Catherine Marshall

Try to Memorize This Verse

I remind you to fan into flame the gift of God.

2 Timothy 1:6 NIV

This is an important Bible verse.
Practice saying it several times. And then, talk to mom or dad about exactly what the verse means . . .

A Tip for Parents: Talk to your child about . . .

Using the gifts God gives

What a Friend!

Just as the Father has loved Me,
I have also loved you; abide in My love.
John 15:9 NASB

Do you know that Jesus loves you? And have you thought about exactly what His love should mean to you? Well, Christ's love should make you feel better about your life, your family, your future, and yourself.

There's an old song that says, "What a friend we have in Jesus." Those words are certainly true! When you invite Him into your heart, Jesus will be your friend forever.

Jesus wants you to have a happy, healthy life. He wants you to behave yourself, and He wants you to feel good about yourself. And now, it's up to you to do your best to live up to the hopes and dreams of your very best friend: Jesus.

Jesus Christ is the first and last, author and finisher, beginning and end, alpha and omega, and by Him all other things hold together. He must be first or nothing. God never comes next!

Vance Havner

Parents Know Best!

Success, success to you, and success to those
who help you, for your God will help you . . . .
1 Chronicles 12:18 NIV

God makes this promise: If you have faith in Him,
you can do BIG things! So if you have something
important to do, pray about it and ask God for help.
When you ask God to help you, He will. And while
you're at it, never be afraid to ask you parents for
help.

When you talk things over with your parents,
you'll soon discover that they want you to do BIG
things . . . and they can give you LOTS of help.

Success and happiness are not destinations.
They are exciting, never-ending journeys.

Zig Ziglar

Today's Ideas About
Saying Thanks to God

Here are two important ideas. Take a few minutes to talk to your mom or dad about what these quotations mean.

Praise and thank God for who He is and for what He has done for you.

Billy Graham

Thank God every morning when you get up that you have something to do that day which must be done, whether you like it or not.

Charles Kingsley

Wisdom

Do not deceive yourselves. If any one of you thinks he is wise by the standards of this age, he should become a "fool" so that he may become wise. For the wisdom of this world is foolishness in God's sight.

1 Corinthians 3:18-19 NIV

If you look in a dictionary, you'll see that the word "wisdom" means "using good judgement, and knowing what is true." But there's more: it's not just enough to know what's right; if you really want to become a wise person, you must also do what's right.

A big part of "doing what's right" is learning self-control . . . and the best day to start learning self-control is this one!

Kid's Tip: Need wisdom? Study God's Word and hang out with wise people.

Lord, What Should I Do?

You did not choose Me, but I chose you. I appointed
you that you should go out and produce fruit,
and that your fruit should remain, so that whatever
you ask the Father in My name, He will give you.

John 15:16 Holman CSB

If you're not certain whether something is right
or wrong, ask yourself a simple question: "How
would Jesus behave if He were here?" The answer
to that question will tell you what to do.

Jesus was perfect, but we are not. Still, we must
try as hard as we can to be like Him. When we do,
we will love others, just like Christ loves us.

Kid's Tip: Want to know what Jesus would do? Then
learn what Jesus did!

Anger Strikes Out

And be careful that when you get on each other's
nerves you don't snap at each other.
Look for the best in each other, and always
do your best to bring it out.
1 Thessalonians 5:15 MSG

The Bible tells us that we should control our tempers. But sometimes, especially when we're angry or frustrated, our words and our actions may not be so gentle. Sometimes, we may say things or do things that are unkind or hurtful to others. When we do, we're wrong.

The next time you're tempted to strike out in anger, don't. And if you want to help your family and friends, remember that gentle words are better than harsh words and good deeds are better than the other kind. Always!

Kid's Tip: Count to ten . . . but don't stop there!: If you're angry with someone, don't say the first thing that comes to your mind. Instead, catch your breath and start counting until you are once again in control of your temper. If you count to a thousand and you're still counting, go to bed! You'll feel better in the morning.

Pay Attention to Your Bible

All Scripture is inspired by God and is profitable for teaching, for rebuking, for correcting, for training in righteousness, so that the man of God may be complete, equipped for every good work.

2 Timothy 3:16-17 Holman CSB

Do you think about the Bible a lot . . . or not? Hopefully, you pay careful attention to the things you learn from God's Word! After all, the Bible is God's message to you. It's not just a book, it's a priceless, one-of-a-kind treasure . . . and it has amazing things to teach you. So start learning about the Bible now, and keep learning about it for as long as you live!

Kid's Tip: Who's supposed to be taking care of your Bible? If it's you, then take very good care of it; it's by far the most important book you own!

Learning to Share

Be generous: Invest in acts of charity.
Charity yields high returns.
Ecclesiastes 11:1 MSG

Lots of people in the world aren't as fortunate as you are. Some of these folks live in faraway places, and that makes it harder to help them. But other people who need your help are living very near you.

Ask your parents to help you find ways to do something nice for folks who need it. And don't forget that everybody needs love, kindness, and respect, so you should always be ready to share those things, too.

He climbs highest who helps another up.
Zig Ziglar

Where Does God Fit In?

Every morning he wakes me. He teaches me to listen
like a student. The Lord God helps me learn. . . .

Isaiah 50:4-5 NCV

Where does God fit in to your life? Do
you "squeeze Him in" on Sundays and at
mealtimes? Or do you talk to Him more often than
that?

Even if you're the busiest kid on the planet, you
can still make time for God. And when you think
about it, isn't that the very least you should do?

Kid's Tip: Find the best time of the day to spend
with God: Hudson Taylor, an English Missionary,
wrote, "Whatever is your best time in the day, give
that to communion with God." That's powerful advice
that leads to a powerful faith.

The Powerful Life

God's Way is not a matter of mere talk;
it's an empowered life.
1 Corinthians 4:20 MSG

How do people know that you're a Christian? Well, you can tell them, of course. And make no mistake about it: talking about your faith in God is a very good thing to do. But telling people about Jesus isn't enough. You should also show people how a Christian (like you) should behave.

God wants you to be loving and giving. That way, when another other person sees how you behave, that person will know what it means to be a good Christian . . . a good Christian like you!

Kid's Tip: Follow a Good Example and be a Good Example: Max Lucado writes, "In our faith we follow in someone's steps. In our faith we leave footprints to guide others. It's the principle of discipleship." Remember: It's not enough to talk about being a Christian; you must also show other people that you're a disciple of Christ.

Stop Fighting

It's a mark of good character to avert quarrels,
but fools love to pick fights.
Proverbs 20:3 MSG

Since the days of Cain and Abel, people have
discovered plenty of things to fight about (Cain
and Abel, by the way, were the sons of Adam and
Eve). It seems that fighting is a favorite activity
for many people, even though it's almost always the
wrong thing to do.

Kids should do their best to avoid fights, period.
So do yourself a favor: try to avoid senseless
scuffles, foolish fights, alarming arguments, and
constant conflicts. You'll be glad you did . . . and so
will God.

Kid's Tip: Tempted to fight? Walk away. The best
fights are those that never happen.

The Joyful Life

Always be full of joy in the Lord.
I say it again—rejoice!

Philippians 4:4 NLT

A man named C. S. Lewis once said, "Joy is the serious business of heaven." And he was right! God seriously wants you to be a seriously joyful person.

One way that you can have a more joyful life is by learning how to become a more obedient person. When you do, you'll stay out of trouble, and you'll have lots more time for fun.

So here's a way to be a more joyful, happy person: do the right thing! It's the best way to live.

Joy comes not from what we have
but from what we are.

C. H. Spurgeon

Sharing Love and Kindness

Talk and act like a person expecting to be judged by the Rule that sets us free. For if you refuse to act kindly, you can hardly expect to be treated kindly. Kind mercy wins over harsh judgment every time.

James 2:12-13 MSG

Where does kindness start? It starts in our hearts and works its way out from there. Jesus taught us that a pure heart is a wonderful blessing. It's up to each of us to fill our hearts with love for God, love for Jesus, and love for all people. When we do, we are blessed.

Do you want to be the best person you can be? Then invite the love of Christ into your heart and share His love with your family and friends. And remember that lasting love always comes from a pure heart . . . like yours!

Kid's Tip: Everybody is important: Everybody is important to God. And you should treat every person with courtesy, dignity and respect.

Try to Memorize This Verse

I have fought the good fight,
I have finished the race,
I have kept the faith.

2 Timothy 4:7 NIV

This is an important Bible verse.
Practice saying it several times. And then, talk to
mom or dad about exactly what the verse means . . .

A Tip for Parents: Talk to your child about . . .

Living Faithfully

Living by God's Rules

Does the LORD delight in burnt offerings and
sacrifices as much as in obeying the voice of
the LORD? To obey is better than sacrifice . . . .

1 Samuel 15:22 NIV

God has rules, and He wants you to obey them. He
wants you to be fair, honest, and kind. He wants
you to behave yourself, and He wants you to respect
your parents. God has other rules, too, and you'll
find them in a very special book: the Bible.

With a little help from your parents, you can
figure out God's rules. And then, it's up to you to live
by them. When you do, everybody will be pleased—
you'll be pleased, your parents will be pleased . . .
and God will be pleased, too.

Kid's Tip: When you obey God, you feel better
about yourself.

Don't Grow Tired of Forgiving

Then Peter came to him and asked, "Lord, how often
should I forgive someone who sins against me?
Seven times?" "No!" Jesus replied,
"seventy times seven!"

Matthew 18:21-22 NLT

How often does God forgive us? More times than
we can count! And that, by the way, is exactly
how many times that God expects us to forgive
other people—more times than we care to count.

Of this you can be sure: God won't ever get tired
of forgiving you. And, because He has forgiven you,
He doesn't want you to get tired of forgiving other
people . . . ever!

Kid's Tip: The time to forgive is now! God wants you
to forgive people now, not later. Why? Because God
knows that it's the right thing to do. And, of course,
God wants you to be happy, not angry. God knows
what's best for you, so if you have somebody you
need to forgive, do it now.

Try to Memorize This Verse

I discipline my body and make it my slave.

1 Corinthians 9:27 NASB

This is an important Bible verse.
Practice saying it several times. And then, talk to
mom or dad about exactly what the verse means . . .

A Tip for Parents: Talk to your child about . . .

The need for self-discipline

Today's Ideas About Kindness

Here are two important ideas. Take a few minutes to talk to your mom or dad about what these quotations mean.

Do all the good you can. By all the means you can.
In all the ways you can. In all the places you can.
At all the times you can. To all the people you can.
As long as ever you can.

John Wesley

The mark of a Christian is that he will walk
the second mile and turn the other cheek.
A wise man or woman gives the extra effort,
all for the glory of the Lord Jesus Christ.

John Maxwell

Real Love

*For the LORD your God has arrived to live among you.
He is a mighty savior. He will rejoice over you with
great gladness. With his love,
he will calm all your fears. He will exult
over you by singing a happy song.*

Zephaniah 3:17 NLT

How big is God's love for you? As long as you're alive, you'll never be able to figure it out because God's love is just too big to understand. But this much we know: God loves you so much that He sent His Son Jesus to come to this earth so you could live forever in heaven.

God's love is bigger and more powerful than anybody can imagine, but His love is very real. So do yourself a favor right now: accept God's love with open arms and welcome His Son Jesus into your heart. When you do, your life will be changed today, tomorrow, and forever.

*Being loved by Him whose opinion matters most
gives us the security to risk loving, too—
even loving ourselves.*

Gloria Gaither

Promises You Can Trust

Do not be afraid or discouraged.
For the LORD your God is with you wherever you go.
Joshua 1:9 NLT

God has made quite a few promises to you, and He intends to keep every single one of them. You will find these promises in a book like no other: the Holy Bible. The Bible is your map for life here on earth and for life in heaven.

God's promises never fail and they never grow old. You must trust those promises and share them with your family, with your friends, and with the world . . . starting now . . . and ending never.

Kid's Tip: God keeps His promises to you, so make sure that you keep your promises to Him.

Today's Ideas About Behaving Yourself

Here are two important ideas. Take a few minutes to talk to your mom or dad about what these quotations mean.

If the Spirit of God has transformed you within, you will exhibit Divine characteristics in your life, not good human characteristics.
God's life in us expresses itself as God's life, not as a human life trying to be godly.

Oswald Chambers

Although God causes all things to work together for good for His children,
He still holds us accountable for our behavior.

Kay Arthur

Developing New Habits

For every tree is known by its own fruit.
Luke 6:44 NKJV

Perhaps you've tried to become a more patient person, but you're still falling back into your old habits. If so, don't get discouraged. Instead, become even more determined to become the person God wants you to be.

If you trust God, and if you keep asking Him to help you change bad habits, He will help you make yourself into a new person. So, if at first you don't succeed, keep praying. If you keep asking, you'll eventually get the answers you need.

Kid's Tip: Choose your habits carefully: habits are easier to make than they are to break, so be careful!

Be Hopeful

We have this hope—like a sure and firm anchor of
the soul—that enters the inner sanctuary
behind the curtain.

Hebrews 6:19 Holman CSB

Are you a hope-filled kid? Hopefully so! When you
stop to think about it, you have lots of reasons
to be hopeful: God loves you, your family loves you,
and you've got a very bright future ahead of you. So
trust God, and be hopeful. When you do, you'll be a
happier person . . . and God will smile.

If you want purpose and meaning and satisfaction
and fulfillment and peace and hope and joy and
abundant life that lasts forever, look to Jesus.

Anne Graham Lotz

Kid's Tip: Don't give up hope: Other people have
experienced the same kind of hard times you may be
experiencing now. They made it, and so can you.

ur Family Has Rules

how we are sure that we have come
to know Him: by keeping His commands.

1 John 2:3 Holman CSB

Face facts: your family has rules . . . rules that you're not supposed to break.

If you're old enough to know right from wrong, then you're old enough to do something about it. In other words, you should always try to obey your family's rules.

How can you tell "the right thing" from "the wrong thing"? By listening carefully to your parents, that's how.

The more self-control you have, the easier it is to obey your parents. Why? Because, when you learn to think first and do things next, you avoid making silly mistakes. So here's what you should do: First, slow down long enough to listen to your parents. Then, do the things that you know your parents want you to do.

Face facts: your family has rules . . . and it's better for everybody when you obey them.

Life Is a Gift

Live full lives, full in the fullness of God.
God can do anything, you know—far more than
you could ever imagine or guess or request in
your wildest dreams! He does it not by
pushing us around but by working within us,
his Spirit deeply and gently within us.

Ephesians 3:19-20 MSG

Life is a gift from God. Your job is unwrap that gift, to use it wisely, and to give thanks to the Giver.

Are you going to treat this day (and every one hereafter) as a special gift to be enjoyed and celebrated? You should—and if you really want to please God, that's exactly what you will do.

Kid's Tip: Slow down to marvel at the beauty of God's glorious creation.

Try to Memorize This Verse

Good people's words will help many others.

Proverbs 10:21 NCV

This is an important Bible verse.
Practice saying it several times. And then, talk to
mom or dad about exactly what the verse means . . .

A Tip for Parents: Talk to your child about . . .

Helping others

Obedience Leads to Hap

You are young, but do not let anyone treat you as if you were not important. Be an example to show the believers how they should live. Show them with your words, with the way you live, with your love, with your faith, and with your pure life.

1 Timothy 4:12 ICB

Do you want to be happy? Then you should learn to obey your parents and your teachers. And, of course, you should also learn to obey God. When you do, you'll discover that happiness goes hand-in-hand with good behavior.

The happiest people do not misbehave; the happiest people are not cruel or greedy. The happiest people don't disobey their parents, their teachers, or their Father in heaven. The happiest people are those who obey the rules . . .

And it's up to you to make sure that you're one of those happy people.

Kid's Tip: When should you get tired of obeying God? The answer to that question is simple: Never!

Be Still

Knowing God leads to self-control.
Self-control leads to patient endurance,
and patient endurance leads to godliness.
2 Peter 1:6 NLT

Psalm 37:7 makes it clear that we should "Be still before the Lord and wait patiently for Him" (NIV). But sometimes it's hard to sit still, and sometimes it's even harder to be patient! No matter. God wants us to be patient, and we must obey Him or suffer the consequences.

We should be patient with our families, with our friends, and with ourselves . . . especially with ourselves.

Kid's Tip: Take a deep breath, a very deep breath: if you think you're about to say or do something you'll regret later, slow down and take a deep breath, or two deep breaths, or ten, or . . . well you get the idea.

Today's Ideas About
Pleasing God

Here are two important ideas. Take a few minutes
to talk to your mom or dad about what these
quotations mean.

You will get untold flak for prioritizing
God's revealed and present will
for your life over man's . . .
but, boy, is it worth it.

Beth Moore

Make God's will the focus of your life
day by day. If you seek to please Him
and Him alone, you'll find yourself
satisfied with life.

Kay Arthur

Don't Have to Be Perfect

...e blessed when you're content with just
who you are—no more, no less.
That's the moment you find yourselves proud owners
of everything that can't be bought.

Matthew 5:5 MSG

When God made you, he gave you special talents and opportunities that are yours and yours alone. That means you're a very special, one-of-a-kind person, but that doesn't mean that you should expect to be perfect. After all, only one earthly being ever lived life to perfection, and He was, of course, Jesus. And Jesus loves you even when you're not perfect. Your parents feel the same way. And if all those people love you, you should love yourself, too.

The happiest people in the world are not those
who have no problems, but the people
who have learned to live with those things
that are less than perfect.

James Dobson

Need More Patience?
Pray About It!

For the eyes of the Lord are over the righteous,
and his ears are open unto their prayers: but
the face of the Lord is against them that do evil.

1 Peter 3:12 KJV

Would you like to become a more patient person? Then pray about it. Would you like to learn how to use better self-control? Then pray about it. Are you tempted to throw a temper tantrum? Pray about it.

Whenever you pray about something, God hears your prayer . . . and He can help. So don't worry about things; pray about them. God is waiting . . . and listening!

Kid's Tip: Even when prayer does not change your circumstances, prayer is essential because it changes you.

Try to Memorize This Verse

In everything set them an example by doing what is good.

Titus 2:7 NIV

This is an important Bible verse.
Practice saying it several times. And then, talk to
mom or dad about exactly what the verse means . . .

A Tip for Parents: Talk to your child about . . .

Setting a good example

Today's Ideas About Teachers

Here are two important ideas. Take a few minutes to talk to your mom or dad about what these quotations mean.

Let us look upon our children; let us love them and train them as children of the covenant and children of the promise. These are the children of God.

Andrew Murray

Their little minds had a thousand hands reaching and grabbing for everything they could see (not unlike their physical hands). A parent-teacher's job is to guide as much as possible what the hands of their minds grab and store.

Beth Moore

Only One You

To acquire wisdom is to love oneself;
people who cherish understanding will prosper.

Proverbs 19:8 NLT

How many people in the world are exactly like you? Only one—the person you see every time you look in the mirror. In other words, the only person in the world who's exactly like you . . . IS YOU! And that means you're special: special to God, special to your family, special to your friends, and a special addition to God's wonderful world!

The Bible says that God made you in "an amazing and wonderful way." So the next time that you start feeling like you don't measure up, remember this: when God made all the people of the earth, He only made one you. And that means you're a V.I.P. And what is a V.I.P.?

A "Very Important Person," of course.

Kid's Tip: Accept God's love . . . and love God in return. God loves you for who you are, not because of the things you've done. So open your heart to God's love . . . when you do, you'll feel better about everything, including yourself.

Sharing with Your Family

A person who gives to others will get richer.
Whoever helps others will himself be helped.

Proverbs 11:25 ICB

A good place to start sharing is at home—but it isn't always an easy place to start. Sometimes, especially when we're tired or mad, we don't treat our family members as nicely as we should. And that's too bad!

Do you have brothers and sisters? Or cousins? If so, you're lucky.

Sharing your things—without whining or complaining—is a wonderful way to show your family that you love them. So the next time a brother or sister or cousin asks to borrow something, say "yes" without getting mad. It's a great way to say, "I love you."

What is your focus today? Joy comes when it is Jesus first, others second . . . then you.

Kay Arthur

Amazing Talents!

> ...e are varieties of gifts,
> ...ame Spirit. And there are varieties of
> ministries, and the same Lord.
>
> 1 Corinthians 12:4-5 NASB

Face facts: you've got very special talents, talents that have been given to you by God. So here's a question: will you use your talents or not? God wants you to use your talents to become a better person and a better Christian. And that's what you should want for yourself.

As you're trying to figure out exactly what you're good at, be sure and talk about it with your parents. They can help you decide how best to use and improve the gifts God has given you.

Kid's Tip: God gives you talents for a reason: to use them.

Directing Your T...

Set your minds on wh...
not on what is on the ear...

Colossians 3:2 Holman CSB

Do you direct your thoughts toward things that are honorable, true, and uplifting? The Bible says that you should. Do you lift your hopes and your prayers to God many times each day? The Bible says that you should. Do you turn away from bad thoughts and bad people? The Bible says that you should.

The Bible instructs you to guard your thoughts against things that are hurtful or wrong. And when you turn away from the bad and turn instead toward God and His Son Jesus, you will be protected and you will be blessed.

Kid's Tip: Good thoughts create good deeds. Good thoughts lead to good deeds and bad thoughts lead elsewhere. So guard your thoughts accordingly.

Today's Ideas About
Waiting Your Turn

Here are two important ideas. Take a few minutes
to talk to your mom or dad about what these
quotations mean.

There is no place for faith if we expect
God to fulfill immediately
what he promises.

John Calvin

Waiting on God brings us to
the journey's end quicker than our feet.

Mrs. Charles E. Cowman

Real Faith

But whoever keeps His word, truly in him the love of God is perfected. This is how we know we are in Him: the one who says he remains in Him should walk just as He walked.

1 John 2:5-6 Holman CSB

Jesus wants to have a real relationship with you. Are you willing to have a radical relationship with Him? Unless you can answer this question with a resounding "Yes," you may miss out on some wonderful things.

This day offers yet another opportunity to behave yourself like a real Christian. When you do, God will guide your steps and bless your endeavors . . . forever.

Kid's Tip: If you want to be a little more like Christ . . . learn about His teachings, follow in His footsteps, and obey His commandments.

A Pure Heart

Keep your eyes focused on what is right,
and look straight ahead to what is good.

Proverbs 4:25 NCV

Where does a good attitude begin? It starts in our hearts and works its way out from there. Jesus taught us that a pure heart is a wonderful blessing. It's up to each of us to fill our hearts with love for God, love for Jesus, and love for all people. When we do, good things happen.

Sometimes, of course, we don't feel much like feeling good. Sometimes, when we're tired, or frustrated, or angry, we simply don't want to have a good attitude. On those days when we're feeling bad, it's time to calm down . . . and rest up.

Do you want to be the best person you can be? Then you shouldn't grow tired of doing the right things . . . and you shouldn't ever grow tired of thinking the right thoughts.

Kid's Tip: Learn about Jesus and His attitude. Then try and do what Jesus would do.

Inside Out

God does not see the same way people see.
People look at the outside of a person,
but the Lord looks at the heart.

1 Samuel 16:7 NCV

Other people see you from the outside, and sometimes people will judge you by the way you look. But God doesn't care how you look on the outside. Why? Because God is wiser than that; God cares about what you are on the inside—God sees your heart.

If you're like most people, you'll worry a little bit about the way you look (or maybe you worry a lot about it). But please don't worry too much about your appearance!

How you look on the outside isn't important . . . but how you feel on the inside is important. So don't worry about trying to impress other people. Instead of trying to impress other kids, try to impress God by being the best person you can be.

Kid's Tip: Beauty on the outside isn't important . . . beauty on the inside is.

Choices Matter

should want most is God's kingdom
and doing what God wants. Then all these other
things you need will be given to you.

Matthew 6:33 NCV

There's really no way to get around it: choices
matter. If you make good choices, good things
will usually happen to you. And if you make bad
choices, bad things will usually happen.

The next time you have an important choice to
make, ask yourself this: "Am I doing what God wants
me to do?" If you can answer that question with a
great big "YES", then go ahead. But if you're not
sure if the choice you are about to make is right,
slow down. Why? Because choices matter . . . a lot!

Kid's Tip: First You Make Choices . . . and pretty
soon those choices begin to shape your life. That's
why you must make smart choices . . . or face the
consequences of making dumb ones.

God's Greatest Promise

I assure you: Anyone who believes has eternal life.

John 6:47 Holman CSB

It's time to remind yourself of a promise that God made a long time ago—the promise that God sent His Son Jesus to save the world and to save you! And when you stop to think about it, there can be no greater promise than that.

No matter where you are, God is with you. God loves you, and He sent His Son so that you can live forever in heaven with your loved ones. WOW! That's the greatest promise in the history of the universe. The End.

Kid's Tip: People love talking about religion, and everybody has their own opinions, but ultimately only one opinion counts . . . God's. Talk to your friends about God's promise of eternal life, and what that promise means to you and to them.

Lessons You Can Learn

Remember what you are taught.
And listen carefully to words of knowledge.

Proverbs 23:12 ICB

You can learn a lot about life by paying attention to the things that happen around you . . . and that's exactly what God wants you to do. God is trying to teach you things, and you can learn those things the easy way (by paying attention and obeying God's rules) or the hard way (by making the same mistakes over and over again until you finally learn something from them). Of course, it's better to learn things sooner rather than later . . . starting now.

While it is wise to learn from experience,
it is wiser to learn from the experience of others.

Rick Warren

Try to Memorize This Verse

The righteous will live by his faith.
Habakkuk 2:4 NIV

This is an important Bible verse.
Practice saying it several times. And then, talk to
mom or dad about exactly what the verse means . . .

A Tip for Parents: Talk to your child about . . .

The need to live by faith

God's Power

I pray . . . that you may know . . . his uncomparably
great power for us who believe . . . .
Ephesians 1:18-19 NIV

How strong is God? Stronger than anybody can
imagine! But even if we can't understand God's
power, we can respect His power. And we can be
sure that God has the strength to guide us and
protect us forever.

The next time you're worried or afraid,
remember this: if God is powerful enough to create
the universe and everything in it, He's also strong
enough to take care of you. Now that's a comforting
thought!

The power of God through His Spirit will work
within us to the degree that we permit it.
Mrs. Charles E. Cowman

Today's Ideas About
Obedience

Here are two important ideas. Take a few minutes to talk to your mom or dad about what these quotations mean.

You may not always see immediate results, but all God wants is your obedience and faithfulness.

Vonette Bright

The surest evidence of our love to Christ is obedience to the laws of Christ. Love is the root, obedience is the fruit.

Matthew Henry

Do Good Deeds

A good person produces good deeds from a good heart, and an evil person produces evil deeds from an evil heart. Whatever is in your heart determines what you say.

Luke 6:45 NLT

It's good to do good deeds. Even when nobody's watching, God is. And God knows whether you've done the right thing or the wrong thing.

So if you're tempted to misbehave when nobody is looking, remember this: There is never a time when "nobody's watching." Somebody is always watching over you—and that Somebody, of course, is your Father in Heaven. Don't let Him down!

Kid's Tip: Goodness is as goodness does: In order to be a good person, you must do good things. Thinking about them isn't enough. So get busy! Your family and friends need all the good deeds they can get!

Honesty Is Always Best

It is better to be poor and honest than
to be foolish and tell lies.

Proverbs 19:1 ICB

Telling the truth can be hard sometimes. But
even when telling the truth is very hard, that's
exactly what you should do. If you're afraid to tell
the truth, pray to God for the courage to do the
right thing, and then do it!

If you've ever told a big lie, and then had to live
with the big consequences of that lie, you know that
it's far more trouble to tell a lie than it is to tell the
truth. But lies aren't just troubling to us; they're
also troubling to God! So tell the truth, even when
it's hard to do; you'll be glad you did . . . and so will
He!

Honesty has a beautiful and refreshing simplicity
about it. No ulterior motives. No hidden meanings.
As honesty and integrity characterize our lives,
there will be no need to manipulate others.

Charles Swindoll

The Master Teacher

This man came to Him at night and said, "Rabbi, we know that You have come from God as a teacher, for no one could perform these signs You do unless God were with him."

John 3:2 Holman CSB

Who was the greatest teacher in the history of the world? Jesus was . . and He still is! Jesus teaches us how to live, how to behave, and how to worship. Now, it's up to each of us, as Christians, to learn the important lessons that Jesus can teach.

Some day soon, you will have learned everything that Jesus has to teach you, right? WRONG!!!! Jesus will keep teaching you important lessons throughout your life. And that's good, because all of us, kids and grown-ups alike, have lots to learn . . . especially from the Master . . . and the Master, of course, is Jesus.

Kid's Tip: The Truth with a capital "T": Jesus is the Truth, and that's the truth!

No Secrets

The eyes of the Lord are in every place,
keeping watch . . . .
Proverbs 15:3 NKJV

Even when nobody else is watching, God is. Nothing that we say or do escapes the watchful eye of our Lord. God understands that we are not perfect, but He also wants us to live according to His rules, not our own.

The next time that you're tempted to say something that you shouldn't say or to do something that you shouldn't do, remember that you can't keep secrets from God. So don't even try!

Kid's Tip: Having trouble hearing God? If so, slow yourself down, tune out the distractions, and listen carefully. God has important things to say; your task is to be still and listen.

Today's Ideas About Too Much Stuff

Here are two important ideas. Take a few minutes to talk to your mom or dad about what these quotations mean.

If you want to be truly happy, you won't find it on an endless quest for more stuff. You'll find it in receiving God's generosity and then passing that generosity along.

Bill Hybels

There is absolutely no evidence that complexity and materialism lead to happiness.
On the contrary, there is plenty of evidence that simplicity and spirituality lead to joy, a blessedness that is better than happiness.

Dennis Swanberg

Nobody Likes 'Em

Therefore, if anyone is in Christ,
he is a new creation; the old has gone,
the new has come!

2 Corinthians 5:17 NIV

Mistakes: nobody likes 'em but everybody makes 'em. And you're no different! When you make mistakes (and you will), you should do your best to correct them, to learn from them, and pray for the wisdom to avoid those same mistakes in the future.

If you want to become smarter faster, you'll learn from your mistakes the first time you make them. When you do, that means that you won't keep making the same mistakes over and over again, and that's the smart way to live.

Kid's Tip: Made a mistake? Ask for forgiveness! If you've broken one of God's rules, you can always ask Him for His forgiveness. And He will always give it!

It's Important to Be Kind

I tell you the truth, anything you did for even
the least of my people here, you also did for me.
Matthew 25:40 NCV

The Bible promises that if you're a nice person,
good things will happen to you. That's one reason
(but not the only reason) that it's important to be
kind.

Do you listen to your heart when it tells you to
be kind to other people? Hopefully, you do. After
all, lots of people in the world aren't as fortunate
as you are—and some of these folks are living very
near you.

Ask your parents to help you find ways to do
nice things for other people. And don't forget that
everybody needs love, kindness, and respect, so you
should always be ready to share those things, too.

When you extend hospitality to others,
you're not trying to impress people,
you're trying to reflect God to them.
Max Lucado

It Starts in the Heart

We must be sure to obey the truth
we have learned already.
Philippians 3:16 NLT

An attitude of obedience starts in your heart and works its way out from there.

Do you listen to your heart when it tells you to behave yourself? Hopefully, you do. After all, you'll be happier and healthier when you do the right thing.

So don't forget to listen to your parents. And while you're at it, don't forget to listen to your conscience. When you listen carefully, you'll be obedient . . . and you'll make everybody glad, including yourself!

You may not always see immediate results,
but all God wants is your obedience
and faithfulness.
Vonette Bright

Kid's Tip: When you obey your parents . . . you're pleasing God, you pleasing your parents, and you're doing yourself a BIG favor.

God Can Handle It

Now the God of all grace, who called you to His
eternal glory in Christ Jesus, will personally restore,
establish, strengthen, and support you.

1 Peter 5:10 Holman CSB

It's a promise that is made over and over again in
the Bible: Whatever "it" is, God can handle it.
Life isn't always easy. Far from it! Sometimes,
life can be hard, but even then, we're protected by
a loving Heavenly Father. When we're worried, God
can help us; when we're sad, God can comfort us.
God is not just near, He is here. So we should always
lift our thoughts and prayers to Him. When we do,
He will answer our prayers. Why? Because He is our
shepherd, and He has promised to protect us now
and forever.

When considering the size of your problems,
there are two categories that you should never
worry about: the problems that are small enough
for you to handle, and the ones that aren't too big
for God to handle. — that's all the rest of them.

Marie T. Freeman

Record Your Child's Milestones From This Year

_____

_____

_____

_____

_____

_____

_____

_____

_____

_____

_____

_____

_____

_____